A Miscellany of
QUIET TALKS

by S. D. GORDON

FLEMING H. REVELL COMPANY

Printed in Great Britain

Westwood, N. J.—316 Third Avenue
Los Angeles 41—2173 Colorado Boulevard
London, E.C.4.—29 Ludgate Hill
Glasgow, C.2—229 Bothwell Street

FOREWORD

FOR more than a quarter of a century there came almost annually from the pen of the late S. D. Gordon a volume in the well-known 'Quiet Talks' series on a wide variety of themes. Such has been the popularity of this series that more than 1,500,000 copies have been sold in the course of the years.

Two decades have elapsed since the voice of Mr. Gordon fell silent and a generation of evangelical Christians of all denominations has arisen that is unacquainted with his most helpful and instructive books.

Many in the past, who have made contact with the 'Quiet Talks' series, have found them at once a challenge and an inspiration. The essentially practical and deeply devotional character of these writings has made lasting impressions on the lives of young and old alike.

Hence, in this 'Miscellany', an attempt has been made to bring together in a consecutive way some of the material that has made particular appeal. These themes have been selected as being truly representative of the best of S. D. Gordon's devotional writing, especially in the field of Christian life and conduct.

It is hoped that young believers, as also those long on the way, will find instruction and inspiration in reading these pages and will, as a result, be drawn more closely to the person of the Lord Jesus Christ.

January, 1956

JAMES HISLOP

CONTENTS

IDEALS

Couldst thou in vision see
  Thyself the man God meant;
Thou never more wouldst be
  The man thou art—content.
                    Ralph Waldo Emerson

IDEALS

HOW CAN I AIM HIGHEST?

ONE New Year's morning we walked out to a little rise of ground among the hills of southern Kentucky, and watched the sun come up over the eastern slope. First there came a glow of exquisitely soft, pale-green light, such as no artist's canvas ever showed. Gradually it changed into a golden green, and spread out two long, slender arms to north and south, as though to gather the world to its warm heart, and always hold it there.

It changed again, and kept changing, but so softly and quietly that we scarcely noticed how the change came, and yet we plainly saw it come. The change was chiefly in the rare colouring, from soft green, to a tinging together of green and yellow-green, and then to gold, each blending into each other, as only hearts that know love can blend. And the reaching arms of light lengthened, and kept lengthening, as though tenderly eager to take in the whole earth and fill it with brightness and warmth.

As the light increased, the central spot on the horizon whence it all came, grew into such a blaze of fiery light that our eyes were bothered quite a bit. The glory was too great for them to gaze fully upon it, and involuntarily we half closed them and turned our faces to one side. And the Damascus traveller's phrase, in the story of another light, came vividly to mind: 'When I could not see for the glory of that light.' Ambitions that had gripped lost their tenacious clutch upon his heart as the glory of *that* light flooded his face. Pet plans blurred and faded, and then slipped out of sight; evil passions lost the heat of their flame; and temptations lost their power

9

to attract and sway, as the beauty and splendour of this new glory threw its wondrous light into his eyes and heart.

And a bit of prayer came quickly up from heart to lip that this other light, that in its transforming beauty was so much above the shining of the sunlight, might affect our eyes, too, all the New Year, and all the years after this one had begun to grow grey.

That burst of dazzling sunlight came to us just over a little hilltop, through two big beeches, and a group of small cedars. We knew that hilltop, for we had been up there more than once. We knew there was a little family burying place up there, where precious bodies had been tenderly laid away long years before. And carved stones of grey told bits of the life story of those gone. But the place had fallen into disuse and decay. The stones were leaning over, some this way, and some that, like tottering old men, and some were fallen flat. Small scrubby bushes and underbrush covered the ground. The old fence was badly broken down. Everything seemed to spell out neglect, as though the hands that had once lovingly laid these away, had themselves lost their cunning and life, and in turn had been laid away. The old burying-place was forgotten. We knew well that was what the little hilltop looked like in plain prosaic daylight, close to.

But, do you know, all that was changed to our eyes as we looked out over the hill, and through its ragged crown of trees at the blaze of glory beyond. The rising sun idealized the neglected hilltop. It was beautiful, with a real rare beauty, as it stood bathed in the early light of the New Year's first morning. All the sharp jaggedness was softened. The halo of the sun was over broken fence and neglected graves. And as we looked we didn't think of the decay, but of the beauty. The decay had passed out of our thought. The beauty swayed us. It seemed prophetic of a new life that would come some day to the hill, and that had already come to the former tenants of those laid-away bodies, and would some glad day come to the bodies themselves, too.

As we turned about to retrace our steps, more of the idealizing beauty of the light came to view. Just below us a bit lay a little group of negro cabins. We knew them, too, and what they looked like in full daylight, close up; for an errand had carried us there only the day before. The unkempt yards, the broken-down fences patched up with things not originally in the architect's plan for a fence, the familiar rootings of black swine in unabashed closeness of touch to cabin and children, untidy garments, untrained speech, and narrow prejudices—all combined to make a rather unattractive picture, relieved only by the ever present charm of human life, from which the touch of God's gracious hand is never absent.

That was what we knew was down there. But it wasn't what we saw now under the transforming touch of the early morning light. The scene took on something of the beauty of the light of God that shone upon it. The light that softened the rough exterior of the cabins made us think of the caressing hand of God upon the lives within. We remembered that God was not thinking of crude speech, nor ragged outside, nor narrow prejudices, but of the human lives that under His touch could be so transformed.

A bit later the sky changed. There were clouds, and they played well their part. For clouds are God's reflectors; they catch the light, and spread out its great beauty before our sight. They are meant to brighten and soften, not to darken. This is true of all clouds, those up in the sky, and those in the sky of your life; though so many have never learned how to look at clouds, and so miss so much. Our New Year's clouds caught the yellow glory-light, and played the chemist for us changing it to a wondrous rose-colour.

It seemed as if all the native sweet-brier of England, and all the wild roses of our own land had been absorbed into one great flood of rose-colour. And as we watched we thought—yes, we were sure, it was no fancy—there was a fragrance in the air, so fresh and soft and sweet, blowing in our faces; and we knew they were really roses, the roses of life, the flowers of God, up yonder, though unlisted in the cruder botany of our school-books.

Then we came back to the town, to the commonplace round that fills up a part of every day for everybody who is doing his share of the world's work. But somehow the glory of the rising sun cast a mellowing light over the commonplace things. And better yet, the glory of that other Light, behind and brighter than the sun, which lighteth every man, crept gently into our inner spirits, sweetening and refreshing, strengthening and breathing in a great peace. And the commonness of the round, still there, and still common, fell into its secondary place, for the glory of the Lord was shining round about us. The rough outer shell of things was transfigured by the glory of the ideal in our hearts. There was standing One in our midst whom we knew, and recognised. And He idealized life for us, while our hands were tugging away at the rough tasks.

God's world is full of things that idealize. The less distinct lights, dawnlight and twilight, starlight and the bewitching moonlight, cast a rare spell over nature. The snow gently covers up earth's rough, unkempt places with its soft clinging white. The green mantle does the same kindly service during the other half of the year.

Distance has a peculiar power to close our eyes partly so that only the pleasing outlines are seen. The artist has caught the same fine touch from the hand of God. How a picture idealizes, whether in paint or water-colour, or made by the touch of the sun upon the photographer's chemicals! The halo of the ideal glamours over every poverty-stricken corner, and every crude and coarse surface.

So, too, God has taught the human heart to idealize. For nothing can exceed or equal the power of love to see the ideal, and be gripped and swayed by it. The neighbour sees a freckled-faced, short-nosed boy, but the mother sees only a face of beauty, and out of its eye looks a *man*, who is going to help shape, and maybe shake the world. The inspector at Ellis Island sees only a couple of bundles being tugged and lugged along by some skirts and a bright-coloured shawl, but the young husband impatiently waiting at the gate, whose hard-earned savings have brought her over, sees the winsome maiden whose face still holds him in thrall.

So the inspiring vision of God comes over all life. The idealizing of the outer world is one of God's ways of teaching us to see the beauty and fineness that lie hidden in the uncouth and rough and commonplace; the victory that waits our grasp within every difficulty. It spells out for us the great simple secret Paul had learned: while we look not at the things that are seen, but at the things that are not seen; for the things that are seen are often coarse and commonplace and are only for a passing hour; but the things that are not seen are full of beauty and power, and last forever.

The God-touched eye sees through fog and smoke to the unseen harbour beyond. It insists on steering steady and straight regardless of the storm overhead, and the

rock or snag underneath. There is a victory in hiding in
every knotty difficulty. Every trying circumstance contains a song of gladness waiting to be freed by our touch.
Each disheartening condition can be made to grow
roses.

Every man you meet has the image of God upon his
face, though so often blurred and marred. Jesus saw a
pure redeemed life in the Sychar outcast, and then
released it out into blessed messenger service for Himself
in her native town. The Jesus-taught man learns to look
quickly through soil and sin to the human life within,
waiting the transforming touch of sympathy and help. In
one of his books, *Salted with Fire*, George MacDonald
tells of a young woman who had been led astray. A
warm-hearted minister found her one night on his door-
step, and guessing her story, brought her into his home.
His little daughter upstairs with her mother asked,
'Mamma, who is it Papa has in the library?' And the wise
mother quietly replied, 'It is an angel, dear, who has lost
her way, and Papa is telling her the way back.' There are
a great many all around us needing the same seeing eye
and warm hand, though not fallen as low as she.

Life has a great holy purpose to be gripped and won,
or done; it is not for mere money-getting, or pleasure-
seeking and sipping. All life is splendidly worth while
because of what can be done. Every new day is marked
red for us in the calendar of God, for what He means it
to bring to us, and to carry from us to others. Each
dawning morning is big and bright with new victory
eagerly waiting our winning hand.

Ideals grip us, and key us up to doing our best, and
giving our best. This is God's plan. They are as the
unseen face of God wooing us up the heights. They
grow roses in our skies and roses in our eyes, and the

fragrance sweetens the air, and freshens our hearts, even while our feet are plodding the old beaten path.

Ideals are God's tuning-forks to keep the sweet music of life up to concert pitch. Tuning-forks are valuable in music because they are so largely free from the secondary, or partial tones. And they are independent, too, of the ordinary changes of temperature. The tuning-fork needs to be given a sharp blow to bring out the tone. The standard of musical tone commonly known as 'concert pitch' is also commonly known among musicians as 'high pitch,' giving the greatest number of vibrations in a second of time of any of the accepted standards. It is rather suggestive, in this connection, to recall that the standard of the French Academy, known as 'French pitch,' is also commonly known as *low* pitch'; and that 'classical pitch' and 'philosophical pitch,' notwithstanding their attractive names, are lower than the 'concert pitch' standard.

We all need spirit tuning-forks, that can be depended upon to give out the true, full, primary tone, when brought into sharp contact with the difficulties of common life; and that will do it regardless of the weather that may chance to prevail, storm and clear alike, grey and blue. And we need forks that are keyed up to God's concert pitch.

It was of unfailing interest in early years, in the old Covenanter Church in Philadelphia, to watch the precenter 'raise the tune.' He always took out his tuning-fork, gave it a quick blow, held it quietly to his ear for a few moments while the children watched with such interest, and then started the singing. The congregation always waited until he got the pitch and began the tune. Although he had been leading the singing every Sabbath for many years, he never depended on his skill or experience, but got a fresh start by the fork every time.

The great Master-musician has given every man a tuning-fork, keyed to concert pitch, though so many are not used. The few great simple ideals of true life are within every human heart; though so often (most often?) hidden away, shoved into dark corners, and covered up by the rubbish of life. God's ideals are meant to keep our lives full of sweet harmony; and they will, too, if allowed to. In the inner chamber of the soul can be heard distinctly the clear sound of the true key, an exquisite sound of gentle stillness, to which all the music of life should be set and kept.

But we need to have our inner ears trained in the quiet time, daily, off alone with the Master-musician, with His Book at hand to correct the inaccuracies of our hearing. Then will come the keenness of ear that will keep us from flatting; or at least, will make us know when we do flat; and will make the sound so disagreeably jarring as to make us reach out eagerly for the true pitch, with a bit of prayer to the Master of the music for His help.

Practical idealizing is seeing the purpose of God under and behind everything that comes, and insisting on getting it out into real life. It was a man who could see through what is often considered an inconvenience, and a disturbance of one's plan, who wrote:

> It isn't raining rain to me,
>   It's raining daffodils;
> In every dimpled drop I see
>   Wild flowers on the hills.
> The clouds of grey engulf the day
>   And overwhelm the town,
> It isn't raining rain to me,
>   It's raining roses down.

It isn't raining rain to me,
   But fields of clover bloom,
Where any buccaneering bee
   May find a bed and room.
A health unto the happy,
   A fig for him who frets—
It isn't raining rain to me,
   It's raining violets.

                              Robert Loveman

The rain storm that may disarrange things for you,
isn't to be thought of in itself simply, of course, but for
the possible good that lies in it. It is a means to an end,
an end both of beauty, and of providing our daily bread.
The inconvenience it may cause isn't to be thought of
except incidentally, in planning to meet and overcome it.
Overshoes and raincoats and umbrellas, and careful
drying-up afterwards, and all that sort of bother, are
simply a bit of the toll of life that we pay for the flowers
we enjoy, and the wheat we eat.

So sickness is a school. It should not be thought of in
itself, but only for the flowers it will bring into bloom, and
the finer strength that should grow out of it. It may
cause sharp pain, an upsetting of all one's plans, and real
anxiety. But these really are only by the way, the bother-
ing with overshoes and other such storm things, the toll
on the road, the tuition fee at school. Of course it is true
that most of us feel the pain so sharply, and are so worried
over the broken plans, and so swept off our feet by the
anxiety, that we are pretty apt to forget the real thing.

It's easy not to remember that the storm carries our
bread in its arms; that beyond the toll-gate the road leads
up the heights into finer air and farther view; and that
school work enriches and deepens all the after life. Indeed,

if we kept these things straighter, and insisted on looking ahead, through the storm, to the blue and the shine waiting above the grey and the shade, we would find the storm blowing over more quickly. Pain could do its work faster, and better, too, and be off and away, if we used it, and worked with it.

> Is it raining, little flower?
>   Be glad of rain.
> Too much sun would wither thee,
>   'Twill shine again.
> The clouds are very black, 'tis true,
>   But just beyond them shines the blue.
>
> Art thou weary, tender heart?
>   Be glad of pain.
> In sorrow sweetest virtues grow,
>   As flowers in rain.
> God watches, and thou wilt have sun,
>   When clouds their perfect work have done.

The tight pinching in money is unhandy and bothersome—we use stronger words while the pinch is on—but out of it come better management, wise economies; and, yet better, keener thinking, and so keener brains for all the other questions that come; keener outlook into life, and a keener capacity for the enjoyment of life, if—you must underscore that 'if'—*if* you keep your eye steadily on the ideal, the possible good waiting your grasp in the difficulty.

The emergency brings quicker-wittedness, and a stronger grasp and use of one's resources, and a sturdier grip for the next one. The practical idealist reaches an eager hand steadily out through all circumstances for the flowers and fruit; and gets them, too.

Is the road very dreary?
   Patience yet!
Rest will be sweeter if thou art weary;
And after the night cometh the morning cheery,
   Then bide a wee and dinna fret.

The clouds have a silver lining,
   Don't forget;
And though he's hidden, still the sun is shining;
Courage! Instead of tears and vain repining.
   Just bide a wee and dinna fret.

Torquil MacLeod

Our ideals change us. They change the face. The refining, gentling process is going on all the time, though unknown to us. The face always bears the impress of the spirit that reigns within. The real secret of sweet womanly beauty, and of strong manly face is here, and only here, nowhere else.

When Michael Angelo had finished his famous colossal statue of David "the giant," many of his friends who had not seen him during the years when he was working upon it in Florence, declared with great surprise that he was changed; his face was changed. And as they looked at the statue, and then at the skilful chiseller, it was seen that he had carved his conception of David, not only into the beautiful white stone, but all unconsciously he had carved it, too, into the lines of his own beautified, ennobled face.

A minister who had been preaching for over forty years, told of two young women he had known in his early life. The one was decidedly homely, commonly so spoken of, but she was a Christian, with the highest ideals being woven into her daily life. The other was a decided beauty, but selfish, fond of pleasure-seeking, and a lover of the gay society that flattered her beauty. In mature womanhood the changes that had come into their faces were most striking. The homely girl had become a positively attractive woman in her face, with its fine gentleness, and its very features refined by the dominant spirit of her life. The other's face had hardened and wrinkled and coarsened, until the word common and a yet less pleasing word were suggested by it.

The creative hand of God is an artist's hand. He planned beauty and strength of feature and form for women and men. But the plan can be worked out only by our earnest help. His Spirit in our hearts works out the real rare beauty into our faces through our actively working with Him. Our ideals will make our faces over into what He has planned, if they are allowed to.

That good word 'ideals' has been cheapened quite a bit in some minds. Or, it should rather be said, that men have very commonly come to a cheapened idea of its meaning. For no good thing can be cheapened, in the bad sense of that word; though we can have cheapened ideas about the finest things. The word ideals is looked at by many as they would look at a ragged tramp at the kitchen door, with mingled pity and contempt. That is because it means something undesirable to them. They think of it as meaning childish castle-building, immature dreamings, visionary imaginings, in the weak meaning of that word visionary. To them ideals mean something clear out of touch with the everyday world of affairs.

Of course, there are plenty of unpractical people who get hold of things wrong end to. There are people who are fond of using the word ideals, but who don't use it in its true meaning. It is made to cover up childish fancies, half-digested plans, and the like. These people are given to talking a good bit, and are apt to use a good many adjectives and adverbs, usually in the superlative degree; everything is 'most.' Whereas the practical idealist is a very quiet, matter-of-fact person, more bent on doing than on talking. Hard work usually makes the tongue slower and more cautious.

These visionaries without doubt make it harder for the true idealist to hold to his ideals. For the crowd on the street doesn't think, and constantly confuses the two. The practical man who quietly insists on holding to his ideals is classed with the unpractical visionary. And without doubt this has influenced many to pull the flag down a bit, instead of letting it fly its fine message out at the masthead. Yet this very confusion and thoughtless misunderstanding make the need all the greater. It won't be so pleasant to keep the flag up. To be misunderstood when one's motives are high and earnest is pretty apt to jar and cut; though some have climbed up to where they ignore and forget the misunderstandings, as they push smilingly on.

Yet of course all this need not keep us from clinging with tight fingers to the real thing, with its fine grain and its rosy hue; nor from the constant uplift of its warm companionship. It should not keep us from doing the crowd the great service of seeing a flag at the top of the pole; nor better yet, from giving Jesus, the great practical Idealist, a clear sounding-board in our lives.

The practical idealist tugging away down in the thick of things knows, and loves to remember, that Jesus is here, now, alongside you and us. Many a churchman, who delights to call himself practical, says, with the air of one humouring a fanciful child, 'That's a very pretty thought'; and then proceeds to shut it out of his practical life. He feels quite sufficient in himself for any tug. The other man who knows by experience how real that presence is, sings:

I cannot do it alone,
　　The waves run fast and high,
And the fogs close chill around,
　　And the light goes out in the sky;
But I know that we two
　　Shall win in the end—
　　　　Jesus and I.

I cannot row it myself,
　　My boat on the raging sea;
But beside me sits Another
　　Who pulls or steers with me,
And I know that we two
Shall come safe into port—
　　　　His child and He.

Coward and wayward and weak,
　　I change with the changing sky,
To-day so eager and brave,
　　To-morrow not caring to try;
But He never gives in,
So we two shall win—
　　　　Jesus and I.

Strong and tender and true,
　　Crucified once for me!
Never will He change, I know,
　　Whatever I may be!
But all He says I must do,
　　Ever from sin to keep free
We shall finish our course,
　　And reach home at last—
　　　　His child and He.

And as he sings his life is full of victory, and of uplift
for the crowd on the road.

Many people think of the ideal and practical as two utterly different things; and, more than different, as opposed to each other. The practical thing to do is not the ideal, they think; and the ideal is not practical. Some go to the extreme of thinking that having an ideal really hinders, for it makes you unpractical, and visionary in a bad or weak way.

There are some who believe in having ideals but don't believe they can really be lived out. To them the ideal is a good thing to have, even as a pretty picture is enjoyable. You look at the picture and enjoy its beauty, but with no thought entering your mind that it has anything to do with your everyday life. Some go a bit further, and think of an ideal as something to look up to, with a sort of dim thought that looking up helps to lift up; but without an idea of getting down to hard work in making the ideal a real thing in life.

If in conversation one refers to the true ideal toward which conduct and life should be pitched, and by which they should be governed, it is quite common to hear someone say, 'Oh! yes, of course, that's the ideal, but, you know, we're living down in the world.' The inference being that it is impossible to have such ideals in practical life; that we must take things as they are, and move along where the crowd goes, and as it goes. The remark is generally made with a peculiar positiveness of tone and manner, as though the whole matter were settled then and there, and nothing more could be said.

Every such remark is a confession of weakness and defeat. It tells a story of knowing the right, and refusing to hold to it, because the crowd pulls the other way. It is a cowardly pulling down of the flag, and surrendering to the enemy, without so much as a decent show of fight. In non-essentials we should follow the line of least resistance, saving our strength for the things worth while. But in the great essentials, we should never budge by so much as a half-hair-width, regardless of resistance. Yet we can smile sweetly all the time, with the wholesome fragrance of a pure life back of the smile. The highest ideals send a fine flavour out into the personality.

There is no greater nor kindlier service we can render to those we touch than the tactful holding to our ideals, out in the contacts of life; whether at the meal hour, in the business circle, in the little group of callers, at the afternoon tea, or the more formal social affair. There are some who exploit their ideals untactfully; and that is not good. Though it is not as bad as those who keep their ideals in hiding, even while they are being abused, and sneered at, and while lower ideals, that are really low ideals, are being freely talked.

But then the cowardliness of some people with really high ideals is painful. The social law that you must be agreeable, and say only agreeable things in social gatherings, leads many of us badly astray in lowering or hiding our flags. There is a cowardly fear of being thought of as a little unusual, or queer, or marked by some oddity. The desire to be thought only well of grips us so. It is true it does take thoughtfulness and strength to speak clearly and positively of the true ideals among those who do not accept them. It takes yet more strength and depth, and real touch with the ideal Man, to do it tactfully in such an atmosphere.

But of course it can be done. And that is a part of the life-mission of him who would ring true. A wisely chosen word spoken in the social circle, where the opposite may be the popular thing, spoken gently with a face that unconsciously fits the word, and a life behind that steadies it, is in perfect accord with the most rigid social canons. It is just what so many need. It tends to bring out to the fore whatever odd remnants of conviction there may be in hiding in that circle.

We need to train ourselves away from thinking that the sweet serious things of life may not properly be brought into any social gathering. The common standards of social contacts to which so many have been trained simply do not make provision for the more thoughtful, serious things. There is always a tendency to being light and even frivolous. The bright, breezy good cheer that properly belongs to the social hour easily crosses the line into the thoughtless and frivolous.

When a bit of the thoughtful does come in, as come in it will, it is quite likely to be subjected to the indignity of brilliant—or, quite as often, maybe oftener, not-brilliant —frivolousness. And that is the sort of atmosphere in which so many have gotten their social training. It doesn't fit naturally into such training to retain sweet seriousness in the midst of the cheery good-fellowship and light exchange of the social hour.

Yet it can be done, and there is no finer sounding-board for letting our ideals ring and sing their music out into human hearts. And no music finds more open, grateful hearts for its uplift and rhythm.

> The robin sang out through the rain,
> He waited not a golden day.
> The gladdest thing that he could say
> Might not be needed so again.
> The robin sent his richest strain,
> Adown dim, slanting lines of rain.
>
> *Edith H. Kinney*

There comes to mind a scene in a drawing-room, one summer afternoon. A group of callers were chatting with their hostess. One of the callers was making the usual sort of frivolous, half-cynical remarks. The hostess was an earnest Christian woman, active in service. We knew her as believing in the highest ideals, and trying to teach them faithfully, and live them consistently. Yet she met her guest more than half-way in his run of talk, not merely assenting laughingly, but suggesting some of the same sort and in the same way.

We could easily see that she was simply following her earlier social habit, that had been fixed before her deeper life had developed. Yet she had both the moral conviction and courage, and the tactful grace of speech and manner, to have drawn her caller easily up to a higher level, through the doorway of his own talk, if she had thought to do it. And what a blessing it would have been to him!

Another similar scene comes to mind. A company of young people had gathered for a social evening. Among the guests was a young woman who insisted on standing on the level of her ideals in any gathering, and with any individual. A young man who had been introduced to her, said, after a little conversation, 'May we slip off to a quiet corner for a few minutes, where we will not be interrupted? For you are the only young woman I have met this evening who will talk thoughtfully.' At the evening's close this young woman and another, a friend, were chatting together. The friend was thoughtful and earnest, too, but with a strong desire to be agreeable that led her to remain on the level of the trifling talk in which she found others indulging. Now she turned to the first young woman mentioned, and with much surprise said, 'I saw you talking with Mr. So-and-So,' naming the young man who had made the request, 'and I wondered how *you* ever stood him, for I was never more bored in my life than with him this evening; I was never with one who could talk so much of little nothings, and be as frivolous as he.'

Each of these, the young man and the second young woman, had high ideals, and longed for fellowship in them; and yet each lacked the bit of quiet courage to give the simple tactful upward turn to the conversation, lest it might not be acceptable. And each suffered a distinct loss, in his own life, and lost a golden chance to help a hungry heart. Whenever one person holds steadily to the highest, others will be kept up by that very steadiness.

The most striking thing to mark keenly about ideals, God's ideals, is this: they have been lived. The thing *can* be done because it *has* been done. They have been lived in one of the worst moral periods of history, and in one of the religiously narrowest and most bigoted corners of the earth.

It seems to be pretty well settled now, that long ago a Man lived, for as much as thirty-three years, who held the highest ideals, and never compromised them one whit, in the life He lived. Yet He was not removed from the sort of life we live. He had to work hard to earn a living for Himself and His household. He lived in a very humble sort of family, where all the testings of ideals come closest home. He belonged to a little village community, just such as most of us know, and live in, or have lived in. And He actually lived His ideals amid such surroundings—ideals that have been commonly recognised as the moral high-water mark of all history.

God is an idealist. And Jesus came to let men see that this ideal God fits perfectly into human life, just as it goes on in every-day affairs. Certainly no one will think that the world was in an ideal condition when Jesus came.

Historians are agreed that it was in about as bad shape morally as a world could get into. And all are agreed, too, that this Jesus lived a truly ideal life, and at the same time an intensely practical life, fitting into things just as He found them.

Though he was divine, in a sense that no one else was or can be, He was also human with a naturalness and simplicity that none other has known, though all may know. That He lived a truly human life, just such as common men are expected to live, that is, with no special gift of divine grace beyond what any man may have, is clearly shown by the simple but very striking fact that His brothers, brought up in the same family, did not believe in His Divine claim and mission. (John 7. 3-5).

To them there was nothing in His life as they had known Him, such as they supposed there should be if He were really the Son of God that He said He was. There could be no stronger nor simpler evidence of the perfect naturalness of the human life He lived in Nazareth, than this disbelief by these brothers, who lived with Him for years in the same home.

Yet mark very keenly that Jesus didn't find it easy to live His ideals. He was stubbornly opposed in them, both at home, and in His home village, and out in public life. He had to fight for them, and to fight hard, every foot of the way. And it was real fighting, too, with moist brow, and shut jaw, and earnestly breathed prayer. He lived them in the presence of, and in spite of, sneers and criticism and cynicism and attempted violence.

And He was a man, a human, as truly a man as though only a man, living His life just exactly as we live ours. That is to say, He personally made choice of these ideals as His own. He depended upon His own strong resolution, backed by earnest prayer, in keeping true to them.

He maintained them against all comers; just exactly as one must do to-day.

And—listen softly, with the ears of your heart—that Man promised to have the same Spirit that filled Him and steadied Him, come into each one of us, and lead us safely and victoriously along the same well-beaten path He travelled. Aye, and some of us have found out that that wondrous Spirit does come, and does lead along that old road up to the heights. Even though a tear-misted vision of slips and faults, and at times of only partial victories lies behind, yet the ideals are sweeter than ever since they have been worked into real life.

When Paul thinks of ideals a number of things come to mind. Some years before his Master had walked this scene—a Man—a perfect Man—God's Man. In the footprints of that Man he must place his feet even though His were nail-pierced feet. Appreciating that he is not a Christian by chance he must 'apprehend that for which he had been apprehended of Christ Jesus' (Phil. 3. 12), and so to the end of his life he finds himself pressing 'toward the mark for the prize of the high calling of God in Christ Jesus' (Phil. 3. 14). And when poised in contemplation between life and death, he thinks only of the highest of which he will never be ashamed and thus does he see:

'LIFE is CHRIST; DEATH is GAIN' (Phil. 1. 21).

Have you ever really appreciated that the outpouring of the blessed Holy Spirit at Pentecost was a fulfilment in part of Joel's prophecy,

> 'Your sons and your daughters shall prophesy,
> And your young men shall see visions,
> And your old men shall dream dreams.'?

And a world without visionaries is a word without the will to venture, without the urge to the highest.   These are sad words of Wordsworth's:

> 'Whither is fled the visionary gleam?
> Where is it now, the glory and the dream?'

What a tragedy if in Christian lives, in our lives,

> 'The vision splendid . . . dies away
> And fades into the light of common day'!

TEMPTATION

Temptation is a suggested short cut to the realization of the highest at which I aim . . . and not to be tempted would be to be beneath contempt.

Oswald Chambers

TEMPTATION

HOW SHALL I KNOW IT?

A DISGUISE is a lie. Its purpose is to deceive. It is something bad hiding its face behind something good. The bad of itself would not have any chance if it came barefaced. It would be refused admittance at once. And if it insisted on getting in would be turned out vigorously. So it steals some good to hide behind. It pretends to be as good as the good. The door is opened for the good, and the bad sneaks stealthily in to carry out its plans.

A disguise is a counterfeit. It aims to make things look different from what they are, and to look better. There are, of course, make-believe disguises used in play in carrying out a part; but these only make it more emphatic that the purpose of a disguise is to deceive.

Now it is a marked characteristic of the tempter that he uses disguises. It is a most significant characteristic. It puts him at once in sharp contrast with God. God is always in the open. At times He conceals His glory. But that is not that He may hold back something from us, but that we may the better take in what is revealed of Himself. Too much light blinds, and the blinded eyes get nothing. A carefully shaded light, restraining the excessive brightness, enables us to see more, and to know what we can't see by what we do see. God is always in the open. Our Lord Jesus said to His accusers, 'I have spoken openly.' He was contrasting His openness with the secrecy with which they stole upon Him under cover of night to arrest Him, and which also marked His trial.

Satan works under cover. It is immensely suggestive

of his character and purposes. In Eden he came behind the covering of the most intelligent and beautiful of all the lower animal creation. He is seldom mentioned by name in the Old Testament. That is a bit of the faithfulness of its description of things as they actually are. He carefully conceals his personality, but his disguises can be found all through the Book, and all through the book of life. His footprints are easily found in every roadway of life.

In the story of Job, it is noteworthy that Job supposed that all the suffering that came had been sent directly by God. It is true that it had been allowed by God, for a purpose, but it had not been sent by Him. But so skilfully had the actual instigator of Job's troubles worked, that the suffering man actually mistook him for God.

The tempter is bad; he is only bad; he is bad clear through; he has no spots of good, nor any spurts of good. He is bold as well as bad. He is as bold as he is bad. He hides behind God. The worst hides behind the best. Satan uses God's roads. He never makes roads. His boldness is startling in its daring. He is as blasphemous in his unblushing boldness as in his unmixed badness.

We want to talk in a very simple way about some of the disguises which the tempter uses. We need keener eyes to pierce through the disguise to the real thing underneath. Satan is a rare expert in make-up. He is deceiving even the very elect of God. He has great skill in new disguises when the old ones are found out. It takes keen watching and habitual praying, much study of God's Word, and a God-guided judgment if we are to detect and avoid his disguises, and yet to be controlled by a sane, poised common sense in all our daily relations and contacts.

Mark first of all this: the tempter hides behind natural

appetites and desires. There are certain bodily, and mental, and social functions and appetites and desires with which we have been endowed. The appetite for food and drink; the sense of taste that appreciates fine flavours; the longing for and delight in personal companionship; the desire to fit into the scheme of life and play one's full part in it; the sense of beauty that can appreciate and enjoy and be uplifted by the beautiful in landscape and in artistic handiwork—these are perfectly natural tastes and desires.

The tempter comes along these natural pathways of our being. He prefers such roads. They make easier travel for him. He seeks to push us to an extreme, this way or that, in satisfying these natural desires. He appealed to Eve's sense of beauty, her sense of taste, and her desire for knowledge. Had he openly told her why he had come, and what the result of her following his suggestion would be she would have promptly turned away. But behind these disguises she was deceived, and so fell into the tangling snare laid at her feet.

The approach to Job was very cunning. The aim of the tempter was to make Job doubt God's love. He came up behind Job's love for his home, for his children, and for peace and prosperity. This was a perfectly natural love, implanted in Job's heart by God. The impression made upon Job was that God was taking away his children, breaking up his home, and taking away his peace and prosperity. The natural tendency was to have his sense of trust in God rudely shocked. The approach of the tempter was behind these natural God-given desires.

In the Wilderness the first approach of the tempter was behind a bodily need. The desire for food was a right thing, of course. The tempter sought to use a right desire to make our Lord do that which it would have been wrong for Him to do, because contrary to His Father's plan at that time. The second approach was through something yet higher up. Our Lord said He would trust the Father to care for His bodily needs. Through that spirit of trust in God's loving watch-care the tempter comes up with his second proposal. Our Lord refused to go to the extreme of a foolhardy going where He had not been led.

Again, the third approach was hidden behind a natural desire. World-wide dominion was a perfectly natural thing for our Lord Jesus. It was doubly so. As a man merely He had a right to such dominion, even such as was given to Adam, and lost by him. As the new head of the race all things had been given into His hands. But He would take possession of His world-wide dominion in His Father's way, and time, and only so. The approach was behind a true natural instinct, the desire for world-wide dominion.

So the tempter is still doing. It is one of his settled ways of coming to us. Along the path of what is right he comes to push us to some extreme, and especially to push us from the narrow path of obedience to the Father's plan, and way, and time. Our safety lies in remembering that every right desire is to be used only for our Father's glory, and as He guides.

The natural desire is never to be an end in itself. It is to be used only as a means to a high end. That end is to carry out God's purposes, and reveal the more His glory. The tempter continually tries to sway us over to using these proper natural desires as ends in themselves. The one thing he is driving at is to sway us away from God's plan by little or by much. It is a cunning disguise.

Then mark that the tempter disguises his approach to

us behind men. I do not mean bad men necessarily. I mean that quite unconsciously to themselves he uses good men in ways that will work out his purposes. That word 'unconsciously' should be underscored. There are four illustrations of this sort of thing in the life of our Lord Jesus.

The first is the coming to Him of His mother and brethren to seek an interview while He is in the midst of teaching the multitude. (Matthew 12. 46-50; Mark 3. 31-35; Luke 8. 19-21). It seems to be a strange incident. It occurs at the time when the opposition to Him by the Jerusalem leaders had reached the aggressive stage. They were following Him up into Galilee, hounding His steps, and trying by every means to hinder and, if possible, stop His work. Their opposition had reached the point of danger to Him. For a second time it is said that He 'withdrew' from the area of their activity. That word 'withdrew' is a significant one, indicating the seriousness of the danger threatening Him. The awful charge of Satanic collusion had been made against Him. This setting of the story should be kept in mind.

One day as He is teaching in the midst of a great crowd an interruption occurs. Strangely enough it is a message sent in to Him that His mother and brethren are on the outskirts of the crowd and desire an interview. It is wholly probable from the records that they had free access to Him ordinarily, when they were where He was. Why this unexpected breaking in while He is at His work? It looks very much as though the leaders had been cunningly working upon her mother heart. They would use her influence to turn Him aside. Surely such a fine-grained man as He clearly is will be open to His mother's influences and to her fears and wishes. It was an appeal to a natural love. It touched the tenderest earthly tie our Master had. He revealed a tender solicitude for His mother amid the pain and distress of hanging upon the cross.

It looks very much like an approach by the tempter behind the tender relation existing between Him and His mother. She, of course, would be wholly unconscious that it was so. Only so can His words in reply to the request be fully understood, 'Who is My mother,' and so on. He evidently recognized the interruption as something serious. His reply in effect is this: 'My mission is not subject to earthly human ties, even though as tender as that of a mother. My relation to My Father is the one controlling purpose and passion of My life.' The doing of the Father's will was higher than any human tie or relationship. It is not the first time, nor the last, that the tempter has come behind the sacred, tender tie of kinship.

The second of these is the story of the enthusiasm of the multitudes over this Man, who could supply bread enough for their hunger. (John 6. 1-15). The violent taking off of His Herald, John, led Jesus to seek a bit of quiet solitude for prayer and thinking. The end was drawing sharply nearer in this event. The multitudes invade His privacy. He patiently teaches, and then feeds the vast crowd with the few loaves and fishes. The crowd is completely swept off its feet by His graciousness and power, and by the sense of inner physical comfort. Their leaders seem to have actually conferred with the disciples, and to have gotten their consent to the proposed plan of making Jesus King. For the Master was compelled to constrain them to get into the boat and leave.

They propose a great popular uprising to proclaim Jesus King. It may seem to us like an immature, weak movement. Yet, if such a thing can be imagined as our

Lord taking advantage of such a circumstance, it would have undoubtedly become a most formidable movement. At any rate it was clearly a repetition of the old Wilderness temptation of world-wide dominion without suffering. Many a Christian leader has yielded to that sort of a temptation. All unconsciously to themselves, the tempter was coming up behind these multitudes in their pathetic need, with the old temptation under new guise.

The third of these is when our Lord first tells the inner circle of the awful experiences ahead to which He would yield. (Matthew 16. 21-27). Peter is startled and strenuously objects. He has the boldness or foolhardiness to rebuke our Lord. In impetuous startled speech he blurts out, 'This be far from Thee.' His strenuous objection raises the whole question of a kingdom without sacrifice, of victory without suffering. It made the road harder to travel. The awful sharpness of the experiences which the Master plainly sees before Him is made to stand out with more painful clearness. It is hard to have one of the inner circle of His chosen band, dear, impulsive Peter, try to block the way that is clearly the Father's way for Him. And the Master plainly felt all of this.

The sharpness of His reply, the blunt plainness of His 'get thee behind Me, Satan,' reveals at once how real was the struggle of soul, as He unhesitatingly presses on in the way marked out for Him. Here it is plain that the tempter was coming behind the warm heart, and impulsive judgment of Peter, who was quite unconscious of how he was being used. The tempter would make the way just as hard as he could. The very boldness of these disguises is nothing short of startling.

The last of these illustrations is perhaps the most subtle and telling of the four. It came within the last week. It is the story of the Greeks' request. (John 12. 20-28). Whether they were actual Greeks, or from a Greek-speaking people of some other nationality, or merely representatives of a non-Jewish people, matters not. They were the outside non-Jewish world coming eagerly and earnestly to our Lord. The Jewish door was in its last stage of shutting against Him. Here was the door into the whole outer world opening. And our Lord had come for a world. He had come not to Palestine merely. That was only the doorway in. These earnest truth-seekers opened to Him the whole outer world. He could go to Athens and Corinth. And how the Greek crowds would have yielded to His sway. But He knew well that only by the red road of Joseph's tomb could He reach Greeks and all the world, in the way His Father had planned.

The language He used shows, with pathetic intensity, how real was the struggle of soul of this Man, now within a few days of the Cross. Listen: 'Now is My soul troubled. And what shall I say? Shall I say, "Father, save Me from this hour?" No, I cannot say that, for this cause came I unto this hour. This is what I will say, "Father, glorify Thy name, even though it mean a cross for me".' It was a sore hour. It was a real temptation. Saying 'no' to these earnest Greek inquirers was one of the hardest things the Master ever did. It is still one of the hardest things for some of His followers to do The tempter was making one of his subtlest, strongest approaches behind these earnest seekers, with their plea for light and help, all unconscious as they were of how they were being used.

These incidents show up at once how subtle and how bold the tempter is in the disguises behind which he seeks to hide his approaches—a tender-hearted mother, a warm-hearted friend and follower, an enthusiastic, admiring, clamorous crowd, earnest seekers after truth. How difficult such pleas are to turn aside our own hearts and experiences tell us, in some part.

Our Lord detected the presence of the tempter behind each. With all His tender-heartedness for His mother, His love for dear Peter, His heart-moving compassion for the multitudes, and His quick response at all times to earnest seekers after light, He still saw that the Father's path led Him quite aside from these.

The tempter has a third way of hiding his approach to us. It is so strange and bold as to make it seem almost blasphemous even to repeat it. He hides behind God! That is to say, he pretends to be God's own messenger. Paul's way of saying it is that he 'fashioneth himself into an angel of light.' (2 Corinthians 11. 14). The boldness and subtlety of this reveals the desperateness of the tempter. It reveals, too, the reality and desperateness of the fight that is on. It is a real fight; no mere make-believe.

The tempter will come to us under pretence of being God's messenger, or of being God Himself. That is to say, he will, for example, quote some bit of God's Word, so thinking to make us think it is God who is speaking. It is true that the quotation is quite apt to be a mis-quotation, or a partial quotation, or a bit taken quite out of its setting, and so away from its true meaning. But it is also true that these quotations of his are accepted by great numbers, who do not recognize the personality of the quoter.

Then, in addition to this is the other method of clothing his suggestions in religious phraseology. There is an intermingling of enough that is true and good with what is bad and not true, as to give the impression that all is good. The impression he seeks to give is that it is God Himself who is talking to us, and so the impression that in adopting and following his suggestion we are really doing the thing God wants done. This may be called the religious temptation. It is his favourite way of approach to earnest, godly people.

It is most interesting that he used this disguise with our Lord. In the Wilderness he preached the Gospel of trust in God. He said, 'Cast Thyself down. Trust God. He has said He will give His angels charge over Thee, and in their hands they shall bear Thee up lest Thou dash Thy foot against a stone.' Was ever preaching more plausible in sound! And was a bit of God's Word ever more pushed out of its meaning in application!

Yet the recognition of this guise is really not difficult. For in it the tempter is always suggesting something a little extreme. The method is really to make some extreme or unwarranted application of what the Word teaches. And this, be it keenly noted, is one of the sure touchstones by which to test his temptations, as we shall see a little later.

It may help to look at a few of his favourite temptations under this disguise. We are taught in Scripture to yield glad submission to God's will for our lives. There has been much preaching of this blessed truth of late years. And many have sought to make this the controlling purpose in their lives.

The tempter's perversion of this is that we are to yield to whatever comes to us, as being the will of God for us. Under that disguise he would lead us to accept as God's will much that he himself—the tempter—sends. The true spirit of submission is an intelligent discerning of what God's will for us is, and then a glad acceptance of it. The tempter's counterfeit is that we should blindly accept whatever comes, as being God's will because it has come. So he would get us to accept his own doings under the supposition that we are yielding to God's will.

There is a vast amount of misfortune, and disease, and mental depression that is so accepted. Whereas if there were a prayerful discerning of what is God's will, and what is not, much that comes would be steadily resisted, as an evil thing, in our Lord Jesus' Name, and so deliverance would come from it. The Master's word to watch as well as pray, if used more faithfully and intelligently, would help greatly. We would find freedom from much that has mistakenly been accepted as from God.

A second perversion of this sort is in connection with Christian service. There is much Christian service that is done merely because it is a good thing to do. The purpose to do good is the controlling thought. The true controlling purpose in service should not be to do good simply, but to do God's will. Doing God's will is always good. But doing something that is good may not be doing the thing that God has planned for us to do. There is a Lord to the harvest. We are not to start in doing the thing that strikes us as being a good thing to do. We are to find out the plan of the Lord, and fit into that. A vast amount of hit-or-miss work, and a vast amount of strength, would be turned to much better account if this do good fallacy were exploded.

Speaking broadly it would undoubtedly have been doing good for our Lord to have met those Greeks, and gone with them to their people to teach about the true God, and to heal their sick, and so on. But we know so well that that was not God's will for Him.

Mr. Spurgeon at one time was urged to accept an

invitation to preach at a certain place. And in pressing the invitation he was assured that he would have the opportunity of speaking to a very large audience of many thousands including very influential people. His quiet reply, as he declined going was that he was not ambitious to preach to thousands, but only to do the will of God.

God guides the prayerful man to discern what His will of service for him is. But this thing of merely doing good rather than discerning the good that is also God's plan for us, has ever been one of the tempter's favourite temptations with religious folk. We should frequently recall the lines that run:—

> 'More anxious not to serve Thee much;
> But please Thee perfectly.'

A third 'Angel-of-light' disguise is regarding that very sensitive stuff called money. The Jews were required to pay a tenth of all into God's treasury. And the giving of a tenth has been widely advocated as the standard of giving for Christians. It is a standard of giving that has been followed by many, and has brought great blessing to the givers, and loosened out much money for God's work. If the whole church membership could be brought up to this standard the Lord's work would be revolutionized in the funds that would be loosened out for use, and immense blessing would follow to the Church herself.

That is all true. But there is more yet to be said that is true also, and that more gives an utter change of view. The giving of a tenth has been taken to mean that we are fully discharging the love obligation laid upon us by giving only a tenth. The Jew practically was taxed a tenth; the giving was not voluntary; it was compulsory.

The Christian is not under any such law of compulsion. He is left free to do as his heart moves him, with very strong motives brought to play upon his heart action. The Jew had much less of light, and privilege, and fulness of blessing than the Christian.

The tenth is an Old Testament standard. But we are living in the New Testament floodlight. The New Testament standard, in effect, is this: that everything we have is to be controlled by the one purpose of telling all the world of our Lord Jesus. That is the passion of our Lord's heart, and is to be the passion of ours, too, as we follow Him. Under this light we are to retain what our needs call for, that being left wholly to our individual judgment, guided by the Holy Spirit, to decide, and all the rest is to be controlled in its use by this passion of our Lord's heart.

There are thousands of Christians who conscientiously give the tenth, and some even a larger fraction than this, and then keep all the rest for themselves. Many of them live saintly lives, are devoted in their Christian service, but live in luxury, and keep the greater part of the year's income for themselves. Yet the millions are without a saving knowledge of the Saviour. And the one passionate desire of our Lord's heart remains unsatisfied, and His return is being delayed. These people follow this course conscientiously. So they have been taught to do. They are on a higher plane of giving than the majority of Christians. They have not gone past their leaders to the Word itself for its simple fuller teaching.

The common teaching about giving a tenth has loosened out vast sums, and, it has been so understood and applied, that it has held back far vaster sums that the Lord meant should be used in making Him known, and in bringing Him back. Giving a tenth has practically been taken to mean giving only a tenth, and that is utterly opposed to the whole New Testament teaching and spirit.

It seems quite a bit startling to say so, but without doubt the tempter's purpose to keep the millions in darkness has been furthered by the teaching that in giving a tenth we are fully doing what our Lord expects of us. It has been one of His subtlest modern disguises in withholding the Gospel of Christ from the vast majority of the human race.

These suggestions give a little inkling into the meaning hidden within that phrase, 'An angel of light.' The tempter has great power of cunning in using religious phraseology. He has fine skill in making use of much of the commonly accepted Christian teaching in furthering his own plans.

And now we want to talk together about how these disguises may be quickly and surely detected. And it is a great comfort to know that even though the disguise be ever so cunningly made up, it can yet be easily detected. It does not require intellectual wisdom or keenness to pierce through the most subtle disguises. The detection comes easily to a heart kept in tune with our Lord's heart. It comes through a simple training of the spirit and judgment by the Word and by the Holy Spirit.

There are two 'hows' in the answer. One has to do with ourselves, and the other has to do with the tempter. The first is in the training of our ears and eyes and touch. The second is in getting familiar with some of the tempter's footprints.

First, the bit about our training. The one need here is to have keen ears, and keen eyes, and a sensitiveness to the evil one's presence and touch. With these it is very important to cultivate a simple common sense, a good poise of judgment. We don't want to move from

Faith Street, on the top of the hill, down into Queer Street on the slope.

The great thing here is ears trained to distinguish between the Master's voice and the tempter's. Our Lord said, 'My sheep hear My voice.' That word 'hear' means recognize. The sheep were trained, by constant contact with the shepherd, to recognize his voice, and to know at once the voice of the pretending thief. We are to be trained to recognize our Master's voice, and to know quickly that other voice that tries to deceive us by imitating His. How shall we get this faculty of quick and sure recognition?

There are three simple essentials here. They can be put very simply and briefly. The first is the act of sur-render to the mastery of the Master. That is made a practical thing by the habit of yielding the life to Him, as each day brings new light. Surrendering is turning every last ragged remnant of the evil one, however dis-guised, out of doors. So only can there come clear keen eyes and ears for his approach. Any unsurrendered bit confuses both eyes and ears. It blurs the moral sense.

The second essential is in the daily quiet-time, alone with the Master, over His Word. It must be daily. It must be with the Word itself. It must be quiet, un-hurried, unflurried time. It must be with the door shut, the outer things shut out, and one's self shut in with the Master. So the mind becomes informed. So the judg-ment is enlightened and moulded. So the whole being becomes saturated with God's truth. Through all of this there comes the sensible poised judgment.

The purpose here is not the Book itself, though it has the central place. It is not even for prayer, though that will have an absorbing place. It is that through the Book, and by means of the prayer, we shall come into direct touch with the Lord Jesus Himself. So the Book shall be enlightened to us. So prayer shall be a real talking with Himself. The Book itself trains the judgment. The direct touch with the Master trains the spirit.

The third essential is habitual obedience to the Spirit's voice as He speaks to your innermost heart through His Word. Obedience has a most direct influence on ears and eyes and spirit. If you obey, your spirit senses become keener, and more accurate. If you disobey, or fail to obey, in something about which you are clear, at once ears and eyes and spirit begin to get confused. Failure to obey dulls and deafens the ears. Listening to what we know is true, but what we won't obey is ruinous to the hearing.

Mark most keenly that the whole purpose here is to get trained spirit senses, so as to recognize surely God's voice, and to detect just as surely the imitation voice that comes. These three things act directly upon the spirit senses.

Then there's a second how of detection. There are certain Satanic ear-marks by which his presence can be detected. And with those I want to group certain contrasted marks of God's presence. First is this: the tempter always suggests doubt of God's love. The suggestion may come direct. Or, it may come so subtly that at first you don't think of it in that way. But as you notice keenly you find the practical effect is to make you hold back because of an element of doubt about God. In contrast with this, God's touch always brings a quiet, confiding sense of trust in Himself.

A second sure ear-mark is that his suggestion is always essentially selfish. It may not seem so on the surface. But if, when sifted down, it proves to be so, it may safely be put to the tempter's account. He is very subtle here.

The suggestion to our Lord behind Peter's objection, behind the Greeks' request, and behind the bread-filled multitudes, was the same—namely, that so He could be saved from the suffering otherwise involved. In contrast with this, God's touch always gives a passion for Himself. And that passion pushes self clear out, so far as it may hinder God's plan.

A third ear-mark: the tempter is apt to be in a hurry. He may at times worry you by a slow, dragging process when that suits his purposes. But he is more likely to try to rush you off your feet with a sudden quick movement. He showed our Lord all the kingdoms of the world in a moment of time. That may be conceded to be pretty swift work. He is fond of sudden moves and of rushing tactics. The serpent's voice in Eden kept egging Eve on to action. In contrast with this, note that God never moves in a hurry. He may move swiftly, but never hurriedly nor hastily. There's a quiet steady on-moving when He is guiding.

Close up to that comes this fourth ear-mark: the tempter's suggestions are apt to make one feverish. This is a sure test for ambitious plans. Any trace or taint of fever produced is a pretty sure indication of the tempter's presence. In sharp contrast with this, God's touch always makes us quiet and clear and deliberate. Our Master's touch still has the same power and effect as when He touched the hand of Peter's wife's mother; the fever leaves.

A fifth ear-mark: the tempter is fond of flattering you. There was the touch of flattery in the Wilderness suggestion that our Lord make bread out of the stones. He could have made bread out of stones, had He been so led. Such a reminder of one's power has the touch of flattery in it. This is a sure ear-mark. It never fails to tell his

4

presence. In contrast with this, note that the Holy Spirit never flatters. He may lead us to recognize properly what strength we have, or what gifts we have been entrusted with. But with that is always the reminding sense that these are from God, and are to be used as a trust, and farther that they are not used up to their best possible limit save as they are played upon, and permeated by His Spirit.

Then the tempter has rare power of producing a sense of fear. He makes us afraid. We hold back because of a sense of dread. Much might have been said of this. The fear that is afraid is a sure index finger pointing to the unseen tempter or one of his subs. Contrasted with this is the fact, just as sure, that God's touch and voice bring a sense of quiet confidence in Him. His presence recognized brings a touch of awe, always, but never of fear. When He speaks we are willing to undertake the impossible, to dare and to endure, with equal confidence in the outcome.

Another unfailing ear-mark of the tempter's presence is a sense of depression, either mental or of spirit. There may be much depression of this sort due to over-tired nerves. And then, simple food, fresh air, enough sleep and exercise, and the grip of a strong purpose, will play a big part in straightening out. But depression is one of the sure ear-marks of the tempter's attack, especially with earnest, godly people. But when God's presence has sweep there is peace and joy. These are characteristic of Him. 'The fruit of the Spirit is love, joy, peace. . . .' (Galatians 5. 22).

The last ear-mark to be spoken of here is one that should be noted keenly, and emphasized much. The tempter is fond of extremes. He pushes things out of their right relations. A right thing pushed out of its right place is quite apt to become a wrong thing. He likes the pendulum swing, first this extreme, then, the very opposite. Truth out of right relation becomes error. Truth is fact held in right relation with the whole circle of related truth. The great theological controversies that have split up the Church so sorely have been largely due to an undue emphasis upon some phase of truth, pushed out of its due relation to other truth. And they have usually been settled by the same sort of undue emphasis. The creeds of Christendom bear witness to this.

The precious Cross of Christ through which we are saved can be degenerated into a mere superstitious fetish. The blessed teaching of our Lord's second coming can be pushed to the extreme of calendar making, and of white-robed people waiting up all night on the top of some hill. And so the sweet truth itself is brought into contempt. Error is flashy and spectacular and erratic. Truth loves the quiet Quaker garb and speech. In contrast with this, it is worthy of special emphasis that the Holy Spirit is a spirit of sanity. No one is so poised and sane in his judgment and actions as the man who is swayed by the Spirit of God.

These are some of the ear-marks by which the tempter's suggestion may be tested. Yet, remember, we are not to be going about eyeing suspiciously everybody we meet. Let us quietly, steadily go on the way the Master points out for us, with our face ever turned toward His, our hearts ever in tune with His own, and our hands stretched out in glad, warm service among the needy. And the Master will guide us safely past snares as we keep close to Him, and push on in His way.

TEMPTATION

HOW SHALL I MEET IT?

A N attacking enemy unrecognized has his battle half
won. Recognition is a long step toward his defeat.
If we know something of the tempter's way of fighting, it
will be an immense help in recognizing and resisting and
defeating him. Our Lord Jesus was victorious in the
Wilderness, partly, because He was keen in recognizing
the tactics used against Himself. His keenness in recognizing made him quicker in resisting.

The tempter has one of two aims in coming to us. First
and most of all, he wants to get us away, and keep us away
from God. That is his first aim, of course. But there
is a second aim, which has not been recognized so quickly
or so much. It is against those of us who are Christians.
No small part of his effort is directed against those of us
who want to be true. And the thing he is driving at
there is to steal away our peace and our power.

There are many who would not do anything they
know to be displeasing to the Master. They conscientiously guard that side of their lives. The tempter's
favourite mode of approach with such is to steal away
their sweet peace of mind and heart. For in stealing
away peace, he is also stealing much of their power. There
can be fulness of power going out, only as there is fulness
of peace within.

And he is also constantly trying to take away our power
directly, or to make it less so far as possible. By sin, by
selfishness in some subtle shape, by attacks upon bodily
conditions, by making us tired, or depressed, or discouraged, or switching us on to some side track, he can

do much to switch us off from the full touch with God, through which only can come fulness of power in life and service. If we are to enjoy full peace of heart, and a steady even poised course of action full of God's power, we must know something of the tempter's fighting tactics, and be prepared to meet and match Him constantly.

Let me begin with just a word about his tactics against us corporately. He is a keen fighter against the Church as a whole. The main thing he is driving at here is to divide the Church. He is an adept at divisive tactics. Under one cover or another he aims to separate one body of believers from the others. He knows the tremendous power there is in unity. He knows so well the resistless power against himself of united prayer, of united action, of a united spirit controlling, that he has done his utmost to kill that spirit of unity.

I do not mean to speak disparagingly of the term, when I say that Satan is a keen theologian. Anything of any sort that divides the Church, or splits up any group of Christ's followers, suits his purposes. And in saying that, I am not now pleading for a universal unity of churches, for unity sometimes means dishonour. Loyalty to the essential Gospel of our Lord, and to His person, will prevent the union that is sometimes thought of.

But the chief thing we are to talk together about now is his tactics in dealing with us personally. And here he has two avenues of approach—he tempts, and he attacks. The temptation is an attempt to induce us to do wrong, to lead us, by much or by little, aside from the one right path. The attack is an attempt to injure us regardless of our consent. He tempted Eve in Eden. He attacked Job. He did both with our Lord. Every weapon at command was used against Him. Jesus met every sort of temptation and attack on our behalf. He was tempted in the Wilderness, and when the Greeks came. He was attacked by that unusually violent Galilean storm; and in Gethsemane, and on Calvary.

The temptation is for all, the attack is for those resisting the temptation. When he fails in tempting, he tries attacking. Of course it is true that the attack itself may become, and often does become, simply a subtler form of temptation. It throws a flood of light upon the character of Job that he was attacked by Satan. Those attacks told this story, that Job had been tempted and had resisted. He had become skilled in recognizing and fighting the tempter's temptations. Then the tempter having failed so largely there, cunningly changes his line of approach.

In temptation he seeks our consent to his proposals. In his attacks he does what he is allowed to, acting within the limitations sent by God, to injure without seeking our consent. So the attack itself becomes a temptation, usually a temptation to doubt God, or to depart from the path of obedience in seeking our own comfort or ease or protection. The attack is really the second hard drive when temptation fails.

In these temptations and attacks, he is sometimes subtle, like a snake crawling along in the tall grass to strike its fangs in when you least think it is there. Sometimes he comes with the rush of a sudden wild storm down the valley, in an attempt to sweep you off your feet.

Now notice, please, the rule he follows in these temptations and attacks. He always aims at the weakest point; that is by weakest I mean the point where he is most likely to succeed. If successful there, of course, his point is achieved. If defeated at that point of approach he proceeds to the next likeliest, and so on. In Eden his first approach was successful. It is rather humiliating that our oldest kinsman yielded at the first point of approach. In the wilderness he went from one point to another, until having failed in each he was obliged to leave. But note, too, that though he may fail at some one point of approach, he is sure to come back to that same point in some changed guise.

It is always good tactics for us to guard our weak points, or our likeliest points of approach. And as a man's strong point is quite likely to become his weak point through over-confidence, therefore guard all points, but especially the weak, the likeliest points of approach.

Then mark that it is a favourite method with the tempter to come through our bodies. He tempts through the natural appetites and desires. He attacks through weakness or sickness or disease. Eve was tempted first by the appeal to a perfectly proper bodily desire. When that temptation was yielded to, the next came likewise in the realm of the body, to use a proper function for a purpose not intended.

Our Lord was tempted first in the appeal to His sense of hunger. It was a bodily temptation. It is striking that the tempter made no headway with Job until he attacked his body. Job remained true through the disasters that came by war, and storm, by loss of children and property, but when his body was touched his strength of resistance began to weaken.

Many a man who would scorn to yield to what he recognizes as a sin in the bodily realm will over-use his bodily strength in doing God's service, or will eat imprudently, or eat such things as are not wholesome, not thinking of these as temptations. But the result is that he is either weakened in his work, or set aside from doing it. And that is, at least, a partial victory for the tempter,

When we come to realize that whatever weakens our bodies is a temptation to be resisted, we shall have gone far in defeating the evil one, at one of his subtlest points of approach.

Another common mode of approach is through the mind. First, there is the indirect approach to the mind. Whatever weakens the body, by so much robs us likewise of mental strength. I know that it has been commonly said that some of the most saintly men have had weak bodies. But I am quite clear that their saintliness was not due to their weak bodies, but in spite of them. If God may have His way, we will have strong bodies as well as saintly lives. There is no temptation or attack harder to resist than that which comes through or to the body.

Then there is the direct approach to the mind. The commonest form here is to make us overpleased with ourselves and with what we have done. Egotism is one of the commonest of all vices. The undue sense of our own importance or ability can get in through a very thin crevice, and does. Yet this is a bit of the very core of the Satan spirit. The line between a proper self-esteem, and an improper thinking more highly of ourselves than we ought to think, is a very thin line, very easily crossed, indeed very hard not to cross.

Only an eye fixed steadily upon Him, who gave us all we have, and to whom we are in debt to do the very best we can with our abilities—only that steady watching of His face will keep our feet steady, too, and keep our heads from getting dizzy, when the path leads up some unusual height, with a crowd watching.

But there are other modes of attack upon us through our minds. And I want to speak more fully of these both because they are so very common, and because they are not recognized as coming from the tempter. Mental depression is a favourite mode of attacking Christians, especially those who earnestly desire to ring true. There is a good bit of mental depression without doubt due directly to bodily conditions. But there is also a great deal that comes directly from the evil one or from some of his numerous messenger spirits.

This depression may be found in all degrees of intensity, from the slightest which yields to help, on to the degree of severe melancholy that leads to insanity, and the taking of one's life. It may begin with a sense of loss of peace, a sense of God's presence being withdrawn, as though He were displeased and had left us. The quiet hour of prayer seems mechanical; the heart seems cold, and these very feelings deepen and intensify the sense of depression. While much of this may be traced to bodily conditions, without doubt much of it is a direct attack by an unrecognized evil spirit who is seeking to rob us of peace and power.

Here recognition is half of the remedy, and if it lead to quick resistance in Jesus' Name, the relief will be complete. I recall talking with a Christian lady from Europe, a highly cultured lady of noble birth, whose service has been greatly blest of God to large numbers, but who was suffering from mental depression to a degree that was painful. Recognition of the evil spirit at work, and resistance in the Victor's Name quickly cleared the sky for the bright shining of the sun again.

Sometimes the attack takes the form of mental stupidity or the sense of extreme tiredness when reading the Bible, or praying, or attempting some bit of Christian service. I recall an earnest Christian woman of much more than usual mental keenness, who for a long time was troubled in this way. Her mind was clear enough with other matters or books, but when she turned to her Bible reading, she grew mentally stupid, and seemed unable to get anything. She would kneel to pray at night and intense sleepiness would come over her, yet when she would rise from her knees, and retire for the night, sleep would leave her eyes. And this continued long until a bit of light broke. She recognized that the evil one, or an evil spirit, was attacking her. And steady resistance in Jesus' Name brought relief which has continued without break. And this is only one instance of many of the same sort that I have known of personally.

I know an earnest Christian whose service has been much used and blest, who was beset with an abnormal sense of tiredness, which held him back from service and affected what service he did. No extra sleeping nor resting brought relief, but as quickly as he was led to see that he was being attacked by evil forces, he resisted earnestly and aggressively in the great Name, and he quickly entered into a new life of peace of heart, and of renewed vigorous mental activity.

I want to say a word here about what is called obsession. We are more familiar with the term demon-possession than with the companion term demon-obsession. Demon-possession means that a demon or evil spirit has been allowed to come in and take possession of one's personality. That was extremely common in the Gospel days, and is still very common in non-Christian lands, and much more common in Christian lands than is commonly supposed.

This other thing of demon-obsession is extremely common, too, though not much recognized. It simply means that evil spirits are attacking and disturbing and annoying us. Demon-possession is impossible without the consent of the man whose personality is taken possession of. But obsession is possible without such consent, because it is an outer attack. And the remarkable thing is that obsession by demons is quite a common experience by the saintliest people, though so rarely recognized. Indeed it seems to be true that it is the earnest, consecrated, saintly ones who are singled out for this form of attack. Whatever disturbance or annoyance an evil spirit may cause in this way, comes under this general head of obsession. The mental depression, the melancholia, and mental stupidity and tiredness, of which I have spoken, really belong under this head of obsession. But it also takes more vigorous forms than these.

I recall the experience of a man of matured years and well-seasoned judgment. He had been led to take an advance step in his Christian life which meant much of sacrifice. He has since then been used in his Christian service in a marked way, and to an unusual degree. This experience came just after the step referred to had been taken. He was awakened in the night by the sense of an unwholesome presence in the room, or rather the feeling that the room was full of evil beings. A peculiar feeling of horror came over him, with strange bodily sensations. The air of the room seemed stifling. He quickly recognized that he was being attacked, rose from bed, and attempted to sing a verse of a hymn with Jesus' Name in. It seemed impossible at first to get his lips open, or any sound out. But he persisted and soon the soft singing was clear and full, and the spirit atmosphere of the room cleared at once. And with grateful heart he lay down again, and slept sweetly until the morning. Yet he is a man of unusual caution, with a critical matter-of-fact spirit of investigation.

A friend was telling recently of a somewhat similar experience. He is an earnest godly man of mature experience, and more than the average sanity of judgment. It was shortly after retiring for the night, and before sleep had come, that a peculiar sense of awful blackness came over him. With the strange sense of mental keenness that marks such experiences he seemed to know that his mind was slipping away from his control. He could not recall who he was, and realized that he could not. He could not even remember his name. There was an overwhelming sense of blackness, as though his mind were saturated with a blackness that was pressing in upon him. And he said he was conscious of being conscious of only one thing—the Name, Jesus. He clung to that, saying the Name 'Jesus' over and over again. It was as though every power of thought and speech was gone save that of uttering that Name. Relief came, and with a sense of gratitude that could never be told, he said, he prayed and went to sleep.

I could repeat many such experiences that have come to my knowledge. These will be sufficient to make clear my meaning in talking of obsession. Evil spirits attack the saintliest men and women, in these and similar ways. Failure to recognize the nature and source of the attack has sometimes led to serious results.

I recall one of the most brilliant, brainy men that ever preached the Gospel, a man of unusual charm of personality and earnest devotion, whose life went abruptly out under the touch of his own hand. The physician used the phrase 'intense melancholia.' But careful study into the case revealed the fact that without question the fuller explanation can be found here in demon-obsession, unrecognized.

These are some of the tempter's fighting tactics. They are given here that we may be quicker and keener to recognize him and his, and so to resist more quickly and successfully in the Name of His Victor, which he so fears.

And now we want to talk a bit on the other side—our fighting tactics. What are the true tactics which this enemy of ours fears and cannot resist?

First of all must come that great statement made of Michael's fight and victory in John's Revelation. 'They overcame him on the ground of the blood of the Lamb.' We cannot get beyond that. The enemy is the same, the fight the same, and the means of victory the same too. It was by the shedding of His own blood that our Lord Jesus Himself defeated the enemy. It is only by that same precious blood that we can get victory too.

This seems like strange fighting, not spear and sword, not gun-cotton and powder but—a Name, the Name of Jesus; a fact, the fact that He gave His blood for us. They overcame on the ground of the blood of the Lamb; so may we. And only so, can we. There must be the daily pleading of the power of the blood, the claiming of its redeeming power from all the power of the enemy. In the thick of the hardest fighting that blood-red banner persistently flung out will rout this foe. We never get beyond the need of claiming the power of that blood.

Then the second chapter in our book of tactics must be this: habitual surrender to the mastery of our Lord Jesus. Only so can there be the fighting that wins. Anything else is letting the enemy within the lines. That surrender must be full and sane and sensible; it must be rhythmic with the glad music of our hearts. It must be habitual, as habitual as breathing.

It must cover the bodily habits, the mental life, the social contacts, the friendships, the business relations and methods, and even that strangely clinging, subtle stuff called money. A glad cheery yielding of the whole life to the mastery of the Lord Jesus, this is splendid fighting tactics, and irresistible. But anything less means loss of power for us, and gain of power by our foe.

Then there is a daily prayer that our Victor has given us to use—'deliver us from the evil one.' It is striking that that is one of the few petitions in the Lord's prayer. It is to be repeated daily, as the language of the prayer makes clear. The old reading is, 'deliver us from evil,' but it seems clearly to be the fuller meaning of the Master's language to make it personal—'*the* evil *one*.' And the word 'deliver' has all the force of the word 'rescue.' Our Master teaches us daily to bow and pray, 'rescue me from the evil one.' It is most significant.

I know a thoughtful man who begins the day by quietly slipping his hands over his body from head down, slowly repeating this prayer, 'deliver me from the evil one, and breathe in afresh Thy own life, in Jesus' great Name.' That is good fighting tactics. It is insisting on all the power of our Victor's victory, in the stress and thick of life's need.

There is a fourth bit in our fighting tactics that needs much emphasis, namely, saturate your mind with the Word of God. Let there be quiet time daily alone with the Book, until you get full of it, and then fuller. Let the Book itself have first place in that quiet time. No book, however good, and no collection of verses, however choice, should be allowed to take this first place. Let the reading be wide, by the page; let it be daily, through the year, with sometimes a bit extra, but never a bit less; let it be prayerful with the heart held open to God's own touch. So will come the familiarity and clear vision so essential. This was our Lord's method in meeting the tempter in the Wilderness.

And this leads directly to the fifth thing I want to emphasize strongly. It is this, cultivate a sane judgment, and a quiet mind. One should pray daily for the blessing of a sound mind, one that does not go to extremes. Nothing cultivates the judgment like this Word of God, interpreted to us by the Holy Spirit. Avoid extremes, both the extreme of over cautiousness, and the extreme of radicalism.

Faith Street is on a hill. It lies very close to two other streets, one at each end leading downward. The one is Queer Street; the other is Doubt Street. You want to avoid each extreme. Live on the top of the hill with clearness of vision, sanity of judgment, and quietness of mind. This will help greatly in actively fighting the enemy. Satan does not like poise, he prefers the pendulum swing.

A sixth point has been referred to repeatedly, but must be given the emphasis of a place in this grouping. I mean this, learn to recognize the enemy's approach, whether he comes himself or through one of his numerous messenger-spirits. Cultivate a keen ear for his voice and step, a quick eye for his hand, however gloved, and a sensitive spirit for his touch and presence. We have heard a little about the tempter's disguises, and how to detect them. That, I hope, will help us in this work of quick and sure recognition. Without doubt our Lord's keenness and quickness in recognizing both tempter and temptation in the Wilderness was an immense help in the victory won there. Yet that recognition came to Him in the same way as it may come to us.

And then a last word must be put in for the hour of stress. When the temptation comes so subtly, and crowds so hard, remember this word—claim Christ's victory. Remember that the victory has been won. Claim that victory as your own. Go in the strength of what Somebody else has done. The victory you are needing just now, when the temptation comes with a wild rush, and nearly sweeps you off your feet at once, remember that victory has been won. It is an accomplished fact. Claim it as your own, and it will be your own in fact. There is far more victory just within grasp than you have realized. Reach out your hand and take as your very own what has been done for you.

That victory has been enshrined in a Name. All the power of the Nazareth victory, and of the Wilderness victory, all the power of the great climax victory of Calvary, and of the Resurrection morning—all is packed into one word, a Name, the Name of Jesus. There is far more, infinitely more practical help and power in that Name than we have dreamed of; certainly far more than we have ever used. The Name of Jesus is the most valuable asset of the Christian life.

I remember a young man coming up to me at the close of a service in London. He told me of how sorely he had been tempted, how he seemed to make no headway against the struggle in his Christian life, until the suggestion came to him of the practical value of that Name above every name. Instantly he began using it, reverently, prayerfully, eagerly, and relief and victory came. And the look of eye and face revealed how real was the victory and peace that had come to him.

A missionary in South Africa has told a story of her experience in the use of that great Name. The story has a simplicity and a power, that makes one feel all afresh that we have not used that great Name as we may and should. She was travelling in Bechuanaland, camping by the banks of a badly swollen river. The discomforts of heavy rains, bad roads, poor food, and stinging insects were very great. But sorer far was the moral havoc being wrought within sight, by the wayside canteen where liquors were sold to the hundreds of poor dark-skinned natives. The distress of the situation seemed unbearable. In her almost despair of soul she was drawn away to pray, then in calmer mood was led to go over toward the canteen.

Her thought was directed to one man, very old, very poor, clad in a few filthy rags, with a bloated face, bleared eyes, and loathsome sores, all the result of his drinking the cheap adulterated liquor kept in the canteen. He was just staggering towards the canteen when she called him. And as he stopped to speak with her, she asked him why he drank when it was ruining him.

With a wild laugh he said, 'Why? I can't help it. I am enslaved by this vile white man's drink. I would gladly quit, but I can't.' And she told him there was a way out into freedom from his slavery. It was in a name. 'A name?' he said with a touch of awe coming over him. 'Yes, a name,' she said. And would she tell him that name. Praying for guidance, she told him as simply as she could the story of the Gospel, and of the power in the Name of Jesus. And the old black wreck repeated the Name, *Jesus*, which was but a new sound to him. And they knelt in prayer among the trees and parted.

Her journey took her away, but weeks after, on returning, she met the old black man's wife, and from her gleaned the fascinating sequel to the story. The poor old enslaved heathen man had gone away, and when the fever for drink came upon him, he had with great earnestness repeated the Name of Jesus over and over. And in his simple speech, the fever left him, the craving for the drink went away, and he felt as if he had never tasted the stuff. He said his mouth felt clean as a little child's, and his body had become strong and well.

One day he had allowed an old drinking companion

to persuade him to go with him. As they started toward the canteen, the old fever for drink came upon him. He could feel it burning within his body. He tried to break away from his companion, but the old slavery gripped him anew and held him fast. Then he remembered, and with all the earnestness of his soul he repeated the Name over, 'Jesus, *Jesus*, JESUS.' And he said, 'A coolness came over my brain, and my body, and I was free again, and turned quickly away.'

The meagreness of the man's knowledge of the Gospel makes the story seem almost startling. But the earnestness of his purpose, and the simplicity of his faith, fully made up for lack of knowledge, and supplied the sure link with the Lord Jesus, and through that link the power came in the hour of his sore distress.

I have no doubt that if spirit beings were visible, any one standing by watching the old black man, would have seen evil spirits hanging about and haunting him, and driving him on in his mad thirst for the drink; and then fleeing, frightened and terrified, before the Name of their Victor, as the old man repeated it, over and over again so earnestly.

The Name that brought the old heathen quick relief from bodily appetite is available for every sort of need, and in every sort of emergency. It is our strong tower into which we can run and be safe. Satan hates that Name. He fears it. All the victory of Nazareth, and the Wilderness, of Calvary, and the Resurrection, are bound up in that Name. And now it is ours to use. The Master has bequeathed to us the right to use that Name, and as we do there is as much and as sure victory for us as there was gotten by Him.

There is a last word that ought to be put in. It should be used as a sort of bright underscoring to all that has been said. It will affect the spirit of all our life, and of all our fighting. It is a word from our Master's own lips. It comes to us out of the darkness of the darkest night He knew. In that exquisitely quiet voice of His He said, 'Be of good cheer; I have overcome.' Out of the gloom of that betrayal night it shines as a bright gleam of light. It stands out against the background of the betrayal of a sacred friendship trust, as a beam of God's own sunshine out of black storm clouds.

'Be of good cheer'—the uplift of its music is immense. Let the joyous music of His victory ring its melody in your soul, and then let the gladness of it out in all your life. Be cheery! Sing as you fight. Be joyous as you push on. There is an enemy; yes, but he is defeated. He is still free to fight; yes, but every fight is meant to mean a fresh defeat for him. We are living on the battle-field; yes, but it is to be a victory-field for us, because of our Leader. The tempter is cunning and persistent; yes, but he is a whipped foe. The enemy is more than a match for us; yes, but he has been clearly outmatched by our Lord Jesus. Cheer up! Fasten the flag at the top of the mast, and nail it there, and clinch the nails, cut away the ropes; the flag, the Victor's flag, is there to stay.

Had Paul seen a typical 'Victory Parade' of first century times when he wrote, 'He stripped away from Himself all trammels of "Principalities and Powers": He paraded them unsparingly, as He haled them in the triumph of the Cross' (Col. 2. 15)? Yes, that is not fiction but fact—the TRIUMPH of the Cross. And in the enjoyment of the fruits of this triumph we may live our lives as overcomers since Christ has conquered.

Then 'Be of good cheer; I.' With that glad ringing cry of cheer, couple the personality of Him who gives it to us

—'Be of good cheer; *I*.' It is because of Him that we can be of good cheer. He is the basis of the cheer. Let this be our constant fighting cry, 'Be of good cheer; *I*—.'

PRAYER

Prayer is not the conquering of God's reluctance but the taking hold of God's willingness.

Phillips Brooks

PRAYER

WHAT IS THE METHOD?

O NE of the most remarkable illustrations ever of
the power of prayer, may be found in the experience of Mr. Moody. It explains his unparalleled
career of world-wide soul winning. One marvels that
more has not been said of it. Its stimulus to faith is great.
I suppose the man most concerned did not speak of it
much because of his fine modesty. The last year of his
life he referred to it more frequently as though impelled
to.

The last time I heard Mr. Moody was in his own
church in Chicago. It was, I think, in the fall of the last
year of his life. One morning in the old church made
famous by his early work, in a quiet conversational way
he told the story. It was back in the early seventies, when
Chicago had been laid in ashes. 'This building was not
yet up far enough to do much in,' he said; 'so I thought
I would slip across the water, and learn what I could
from preachers there, so as to do better work here. I
had gone over to London, and was running around after
men there.' Then he told of going one evening to hear
Mr. Spurgeon in the Metropolitan Tabernacle; and
understanding that he was to speak a second time that
evening to dedicate a chapel, Mr. Moody had slipped
out of the building and had run along the street after
Mr. Spurgeon's carriage a mile or so, so as to hear him
the second time. Then he smiled, and said quietly, 'I
was running around after men like that.'

He had not been speaking anywhere, he said, but
listening to others. One day, Saturday, at noon, he had

71

gone into the meeting in Exeter Hall on the Strand; felt
impelled to speak a little when the meeting was thrown
open, and did so. At the close, among others who greeted
him, one man, a minister, asked him to come and preach
for him the next day morning and night, and he said he
would. Mr. Moody said, 'I went to the morning service
and found a large church full of people. And when the
time came I began to speak to them. But it seemed the
hardest talking ever I did. There was no response in
their faces. They seemed as though carved out of stone
or ice. And I was having a hard time: and wished I
wasn't there; and wished I hadn't promised to speak again
at night. But I had promised, and so I went.

'At night it was the same thing; house full, people
outwardly respectful, but no interest, no response. And
I was having a hard time again. When about half-way
through my talk there came a change. It seemed as
though the windows of heaven had opened and a bit of
breath blew down. The atmosphere of the building
seemed to change. The people's faces changed. It impressed me so that when I finished speaking I gave the
invitation for those who wanted to be Christians to rise.
I thought there might be a few. And to my immense
surprise the people got up in groups, pews-full. I turned
to the minister and said, "What does this mean?" He
said, "I don't know, I'm sure." 'Well,' Mr. Moody said,
'they misunderstood me. I'll explain what I meant.' So
he announced an after-meeting in the room below,
explaining who were invited: only those who wanted to
be Christians; and putting pretty clearly what he understood that to mean, and dismissed the service.

They went to the lower room. And the people came
crowding, jamming in below, filling all available space,
seats, aisles and standing room. Mr. Moody talked

again a few minutes, and then asked those who would be Christians to rise. This time he knew he had made his meaning clear. They got up in clumps, in groups by fifties! Mr. Moody said, 'I turned and said to the minister, "What does this mean?" He said, "I'm sure I don't know".' Then the minister said to Mr. Moody, 'What'll I do with these people? I don't know what to do with them; this is something new.' And he said, 'Well, I'd announce a meeting for to-morrow night and Tuesday night, and see what comes of it; I'm going across the channel to Dublin.' And he went, but he had barely stepped off the boat when a cablegram was handed him from the minister saying, 'Come back at once. Church packed.' So he went back, and stayed ten days. And the result of that ten days, as I recall Mr. Moody's words, was that four hundred were added to that church, and that every church nearby felt the impulse of those ten days. Then Mr. Moody dropped his head, as though thinking back, and said, 'I had no plans beyond this church. I supposed my life work was here. But the result with me was that I was given a roving commission and have been working under it ever since.'

Now what was the explanation of that marvellous Sunday and the days following? It was not Mr. Moody's doing, though he was a leader whom God could and did mightily use. It was not the minister's doing; for he was as greatly surprised as the leader. There was some secret hidden beneath the surface of those ten days. With his usual keenness Mr. Moody set himself to ferret it out.

By and by this incident came to him. A member of the church, a woman, had been taken sick some time before. Then she grew worse. Then the physician told her that she would not recover. That is, she would not die at once, so far as he could judge, but she would be shut in her home for years. And she lay there trying to think what that meant: to be shut in for years. And she thought of her life, and said, 'How little I've done for God: practically nothing: and now what can I do shut in here on my back.' And she said, 'I can pray.'

May I put this word in here as a parenthesis in the story—that God oftentimes allows us to be shut in—He does not shut us in—He does not need to—simply take His hand off partly—there is enough disobedience to His law of our bodies all the time to shut us aside—no trouble on that side of the problem—with pain to Himself, against His own first will for us, He allows us to be shut in, because only so can He get our attention from other things to what He wants done; get us to see things, and think things His way. I am compelled to think it is so.

She said, 'I *will* pray.' And she was led to pray for her church. Her sister, also a member of the church, lived with her, and was her link with the outer world. Sundays, after church service, the sick woman would ask, 'Any special interest in church to-day?' 'No,' was the constant reply. Wednesday nights, after prayer meetings, 'Any special interest in the service to-night?— there must have been.' 'No; nothing new; same old deacons made the same old prayers.'

But one Sunday noon the sister came in from service and asked, 'Who do you think preached to-day?' 'I don't know—who?' 'Why, a stranger from America, a man called Moody, I think was the name.' And the sick woman's face turned a bit whiter, and her eye looked half scared, and her lip trembled a bit, and she quietly said, 'I know what that means. There's something coming to the old church. Don't bring me any dinner. I must spend this afternoon in prayer.' And so she did. And that night in the service that startling change came.

Then to Mr. Moody himself, as he sought her out in her sick room, she told how nearly two years before there came into her hands a copy of a paper published in Chicago called the *Watchman* that contained a talk by Mr. Moody in one of the Chicago meetings, Farwell Hall meetings, I think. All she knew was that talk made her heart burn, and there was the name M-O-O-D-Y. And she was led to pray that God would send that man into their church in London. As simple a prayer as that.

And the months went by, and a year, and over; still she prayed. Nobody knew of it but herself and God. No change seemed to come. Still she prayed. And of course her prayer wrought its purpose. Every Spirit-suggested prayer does. And that is the touchstone of true prayer. And the Spirit of God moved that man of God over to the seaboard, and across the water and into London, and into their church. Then a bit of special siege-prayer, a sort of last charge up the steep hill, and that night the victory came.

Do you not believe—I believe without a doubt, that some day when the night is gone, and the morning light comes up, and we know as we are known, that we shall find that the largest single factor, in that ten days' work, and in the changing of tens of thousands of lives under Moody's leadership was that woman in her praying. Not the only factor, mind you. Moody, a man of rare leadership and consecration, and hundreds of faithful ministers and others rallying to his support. But behind and beneath Moody and the others, and to be reckoned with as first this woman's praying.

Yet I do not know her name. I know Mr. Moody's name. I could name scores of faithful men associated

with him in his campaigns, but the name of this one in
whom humanly is the secret of it all I do not know. Ah!
It is a secret service. We do not know who the great
ones are. Many such hidden ones may yet be found in
our large cities, and still praying. Shall we pray! Shall we
not pray! If something else must slip out, something
important, shall we not see to it that intercession has
first place!

With that thought in mind let me now suggest a bit
of how to pray. As simple a subject as that: how to pray
the how of method.

The first thing in prayer is to find God's purpose, the
trend, the swing of it; the second thing to make that
purpose our prayer. We want to find out what God is
thinking, and then to claim that that shall be done. God
is seated up yonder on the throne. Jesus Christ is sitting
by His side glorified. Everywhere in the universe God's
will is being done except in this corner, called the earth,
and its atmosphere, and that bit of the heavens above it
where Satan's headquarters are.

It has been done down here by one person—Jesus.
He came here to this prodigal planet and did God's will
perfectly. He went away. And He has sought and seeks
to have men down upon the earth so fully in touch with
Himself that He may do in them and through them just
what He will. That He may reproduce Himself in these
men, and have God's will done again down on the earth.
Now prayer is this: finding out God's purpose for our
lives, and for the earth and insisting that that shall be
done here. The great thing then is to find out and insist
upon God's will. And the how of method in prayer is
concerned with that.

Many a time I have met with a group of persons for
prayer. Various special matters for prayer are brought

up. Here is this man, needing prayer, and this particular matter, and this one, and this. Then we kneel and pray. And I have many a time thought—not critically in a bad sense—as I have listened to their prayers, as though this is the prayer I must offer: 'Blessed Holy Spirit, Thou knowest this man, and what the lacking thing is in him. There is trouble there. Thou knowest this sick woman, and what the difficulty is there. This problem, and what the hindrance is in it. Blessed Spirit, pray in me the prayer Thou art praying for this man, and this thing, and this one. The prayer Thou art praying, I pray that, in Jesus' name. Thy will be done here under these circumstances.'

Sometimes I feel clear as to the particular prayer to offer, but many a time I am puzzled to know. I put this fact with this, but I may not know all the facts. I know this man who evidently needs praying for, a Christian man perhaps, his mental characteristics, his conceptions of things, the kind of a will he has, but there may be some fact in there that I do not know, that seriously affects the whole difficulty. And I am compelled to fall back on this: I don't know how to pray as I ought. But the Spirit within me will make intercession for this man as I allow Him to have free swing in me as the medium of His prayer. And He who is listening above as He hears His will for this man being repeated down on the battlefield will recognize His own purpose, of course. And so that thing will be working out because of Jesus' victory over the evil one.

But I may become so sensitive to the Spirit's thoughts and presence, that I shall know more keenly and quickly what to pray for. In so far as I do I become a more skilful partner of His on the earth in getting God's will done.

There are six suggestions here on how to pray. First—
we need time for prayer, unhurried time, daily time, time
enough to forget about how much time it is. I do not
mean now: rising in the morning at the very last moment,
and dressing, it may be hurriedly, and then kneeling a few
moments so as to feel easier in mind: not that. I do not
mean the last thing at night when you are jaded and
fagged, and almost between the sheets, and then remember and look up a verse and kneel a few moments: not
that. That is good so far as it goes. I am not criticising
that. Better sweeten and sandwich the day with all of
that sort you can get in. But just now I mean this:
taking time when the mind is fresh and keen, and the
spirit sensitive, to thoughtfully pray. We haven't time.
Life is so crowded. It must be taken from something
else, something important, but still less important than
this.

Sacrifice is the continual law of life. The important
thing must be sacrificed to the more important. One
needs to cultivate a mature judgment, or his strength will
be frizzled away in the less important details, and the
greater thing go undone, or be done poorly with the fag-
ends of strength. If we would become skilled inter-
cessors, and know how to pray simply enough we must
take quiet time daily to get off alone.

The second suggestion: we need a place for prayer.
Oh! you can pray anywhere, on the street, in the store,
travelling, measuring dry goods, hands in dishwater—
where not. But you are not likely to unless you have been
off in some quiet place shut in alone with God. The
Master said: 'Enter into thine inner chamber, and having
shut thy door': that door is important. It shuts out, and
it shuts in. 'Pray to thy Father who is in secret.' God is
here in this shut-in spot. One must get alone to find out

that he never is alone. The more alone we are as far as men are concerned the less alone we are so far as God is concerned.

The quiet place and time are needful to train the ears for keen hearing. A mother will hear the faintest cry of her babe just awakening. It is upstairs perhaps; the tiniest bit of a sound comes; nobody else hears; but quick as a flash the mother's hands are held quiet, the head alert, then she is off. Her ears are trained beyond anybody's; love's training. We need trained ears. A quiet place shuts out the outer sounds, and gives the inner ear a chance to learn other sounds.

A man was standing in a telephone booth trying to talk, but could not make out the message. He kept saying, 'I can't hear, I can't hear.' The other man by and by said sharply, 'If you'll shut that door you can hear.' His door was shut and he could hear not only the man's voice but the street and store noises, too. Some folks have gotten their hearing badly confused because their doors have not been shut enough. Man's voice and God's voice get mixed in their ears. They cannot tell between them. The bother is partly with the door. If you'll shut that door you can hear.

The third suggestion needs much emphasis to-day: give the Book of God its place in prayer. Prayer is not talking to God—simply. It is listening first, then talking. Prayer needs three organs of the head, an ear, a tongue and an eye. First an ear to hear what God says, then a tongue to speak, then an eye to look out for the result. Bible study is the listening side of prayer. The purpose of God comes in through the ear, passes through the heart taking on the tinge of your personality, and goes out at the tongue as prayer. It is pathetic what a time God has getting a hearing down here. He is ever speaking but even where there may be some inclination to hear the sounds of earth are choking in our ears the sound of His voice. God speaks in His Word. The most we know of God comes to us here. This Book is God in print. It was inspired, and it is inspired. God Himself speaks in this Book. That puts it in a place by itself, quite apart from all others. Studying it keenly, intelligently, reverently will reveal God's great will. What He says will utterly change what you will say.

The fourth suggestion is this: Let the Spirit teach you how to pray. The more you pray the more you will find yourself saying to yourself, 'I don't know how to pray.' Well, God understands that. Paul knew that out of his own experience before he wrote it down. And God has a plan to cover our need there. There is One who is a master intercessor. He understands praying perfectly. He is the Spirit of prayer. God has sent Him down to live inside you and me, partly for this, to teach us the fine art of prayer. The suggestion is this: let Him teach you.

When you go alone in the quiet time and place with the Book quietly pray: 'Blessed Prayer-Spirit, Master-Spirit, teach me how to pray,' and He will. Do not be nervous, or agitated, wondering if you will understand. Study to be quiet; mind quiet, body quiet. Be still and listen. Remember Luther's version of David's words in Psalm 37. 7, 'Be silent to God, and let Him mould thee.'

You will find your praying changing. You will talk more simply, like a man transacting business or a child asking, though of course with a reverence and a deepness of feeling not in those things. You will quit asking for some things. Some of the old forms of prayer will drop from your lips likely enough. You will use fewer words, maybe, but they will be spoken with a quiet absolute faith that this thing you are asking is being worked out.

This thing of letting the Spirit teach must come first in one's praying, and remain to the last, and continue all along as the leading dominant factor. He is a Spirit of prayer peculiarly. The highest law of the Christian life is obedience to the leading of the Holy Spirit. There needs to be a cultivated judgment in reading His leading, and not mistaking our haphazard thoughts as His voice. He should be allowed to teach us how to pray and more, to dominate our praying. The whole range and intensity of the spirit conflict is under His eye. He is God's general on the field of action. There come crises in the battle when the turn of the tide wavers. He knows when a bit of special praying is needed to turn the tide and bring victory. So there needs to be special seasons of persistent prayer, a continuing until victory is assured. Obey His promptings. Sometimes there comes an impulse to pray, or to ask another to pray. And we think, 'Why, I have just been praying,' or, 'he does pray about this anyway. It is not necessary to pray again. I do not just like to suggest it.' Better obey the impulse quietly, with fewest words of explanation to the other one concerned, or no words beyond simply the request.

Let Him, this wondrous Holy Spirit teach you how to pray. It will take time. You may be a bit set in your way, but if you will just yield and patiently wait, He will teach you what to pray, suggest definite things, and often the very language of prayer.

You will notice that the chief purpose of these four suggestions is to learn God's will. The quiet place, the quiet time, the Book, the Spirit—this is the schoolroom as Andrew Murray would finely put it. Here we learn His will. Learning that makes one eager to have it done, and breathes anew the longing prayer that it may be done.

6

There is a fine word much used in the Psalms, and in Isaiah for this sort of thing—waiting. Over and over again that is the word used for that contact with God which reveals to us His will, and imparts to us anew His desires. It is a word full of richest and deepest meaning. Waiting is not an occasional nor a hurried thing. It means steadfastness, that is holding on; patience, that is holding back; expectancy, that is holding the face up to see; obedience, that is holding one's self in readiness to go or do; it means listening, that is holding quiet and still so as to hear.

The fifth suggestion is that prayer must be in Jesus' name. The relationship of prayer is through Jesus. And the prayer itself must be offered in His Name, because the whole strength of the case lies in Jesus. I recall distinctly a certain section of this country where I was for awhile, and very rarely did I hear Jesus' Name used in prayer. I heard men, that I knew must be good men, praying in church, in prayer-meeting and elsewhere with no mention of Jesus. Let us distinctly bear in mind that we have no standing with God except through Jesus.

If the keenest lawyer of London, who knew more of American law, and of Illinois statute and of Chicago ordinance—suppose such a case—were to come here, could he plead a case in your court-house? You know he could not. He would have no legal standing here. Now you and I have no standing at yonder bar. We are disbarred through sin. Only as we come through one who has recognized standing there can we come.

But turn that fact around. As we do come in Jesus' Name, it is the same as though Jesus prayed. It is the same as though—let me be saying it very softly so it may seem very reverent—as though Jesus put His arm in yours and took you up to the Father, and said, 'Father, here is a friend of mine; we're on good terms. Please give him anything he asks, for My sake.' And the Father would quickly bend over and graciously say, 'What'll you have? You may have anything you ask when My Son asks for it.' That is the practical effect of asking in Jesus' Name. But I am very, very clear of this, and I keep swinging back to it, that in the ultimate analysis the force of using Jesus' Name is that He is the Victor over the traitor prince. Prayer is repeating the Victor's Name into the ears of Satan and insisting upon his retreat. As one prays persistently in Jesus' Name, the evil one must go. Reluctantly, angrily, he must loosen his clutches, and go back.

The sixth suggestion is a familiar one, and yet one much misunderstood. Prayer must be in faith. But please note that faith here is not believing that God can, but that He will. It is kneeling and making the prayer, and then saying, 'Father, I thank Thee for this; that it will be so, I thank Thee.' Then rising and going about your duties, saying, 'that thing is settled.' Going again and again, and repeating the prayer with the thanks, and then saying as you go off, 'that matter is assured.' Not going repeatedly to persuade God. But because prayer is the deciding factor in a spirit conflict and each prayer is like a fresh blow between the eyes of the enemy, a fresh broadside from your fleet upon the fort.

'Well,' someone will say, 'now you are getting that keyed up rather high. Can we all have faith like that? Can a man make himself believe?' There should be no unnatural mechanical insisting that you do believe. Some earnest people make a mistake there. And we will not all have faith like that. That is quite true, and I can easily tell you why. The faith that believes that God will do what you ask is not born in a hurry; it is not born in the dust of the street, and the noise of the crowd. But I can tell where that faith will have a birthplace and keep growing stronger; in every heart that takes quiet time off habitually with God, and listens to His voice in His word. Into that heart will come a simple strong faith that the thing it is led to ask shall be accomplished.

That faith has four simple characteristics. It is intelligent. It finds out what God's will is. Faith is never contrary to reason. Sometimes it is a bit higher up; the reasoning process has not yet reached up to it. Second, it is obedient. It fits its life into God's will. There is apt to be a stiff rub here all the time. Then it is expectant. It looks out for the result. It bows down upon the earth, but sends a man to keep an eye on the sea. And then it is persistent. It hangs on. It says, 'Go again seven times; seventy times seven.' It reasons that having learned God's will, and knowing that He does not change, the delay must be caused by the third person, the enemy, and that stubborn persistence in the Victor's Name routs him, and leaves a clear field.

PRAYER

WHAT ARE ITS TERMS?

GOD answers prayer. Prayer is God and man joining hands to secure some high end. He joins with us through the communication of prayer in accomplishing certain great results. This is the main drive of prayer. Our asking and expecting and God's doing jointly bring to pass things that otherwise would not come to pass. Prayer changes things. This is the great fact of prayer.

Yet a great many prayers are not answered. Or, to put it more accurately, a great many prayers fail utterly of accomplishing any results. Probably it is accurate to say that thousands of prayers go up and bring nothing down. This is certainly true. Let us say it just as bluntly and plainly as it can be said. As a result many persons are saying: 'Well, prayer is not what you claim for it: we prayed and no answer came: nothing was changed.'

From all sorts of circles, and in all sorts of language comes this statement. Scholarly men who write with wisdom's words, and thoughtless people whose thinking never even pricks the skin of the subject, and all sorts of people in between group themselves together here. And they are right, quite right. The bother is that what they say is not all there is to be said. There is yet more to be said, that is right, too, and that changes the final conclusion radically. Partial truth is a very mean sort of lie.

The prayer plan like many another has been much disturbed, and often broken. And one who would be a partner with God up to the limit of his power must understand the things that hinder the prayer plan. There are three sorts of hindrances to prayer. First of all there are things in us that break off connection with God, the source of the changing power. Then there are certain things in us that delay, or diminish the results; that interfere with the full swing of the prayer plan of operations. And then there is a great outside hindrance to be reckoned upon. We want to talk together of the first of these, namely, the hindrances that break off connections between God and His human partner.

Here again there is a division into three. There are three things directly spoken of in the book of God that hinder prayer. One of these is a familiar thing. What a pity that repugnant things may become so familiar as no longer to repel. It is this:—sin hinders prayer. In Isaiah's first chapter God Himself speaking says, 'When you stretch out your hands'—the way they prayed, standing with outstretched hands—'I will shut My eyes; when you make many prayers, I will shut My ears.' (Isaiah 1. 15). Why? What's the difficulty? These outstretched hands are soiled! They are actually holding their sin-soiled hands up into God's face; and He is compelled to look at the thing most hateful to Him. In the fifty-ninth chapter of this same book, God Himself is talking again. Listen, 'Behold! the Lord's hand is not shortened: His ear is not heavy.' There is no trouble on the up side. God is all right. 'But'—listen with both your ears—'your iniquities . . . your sins . . . your hands . . . your fingers . . . your lips . . . your tongue . . .' the slime of sin is oozing over everything! Turn back to that sixty-sixth Psalm—'if I regard iniquity in my heart the Lord will not hear me.' How much more if the sin of the heart get into the hands or the life! And the fact to put down plainly in blackest ink once for all is this—sin hinders prayer. There is nothing surprising about this. That we can think the reverse is the surprising thing. Prayer is transacting business with God. Sin is breaking with God.

Suppose I had a private wire from my apartments here to my home in Cleveland, and some one should go outside and drag the wire down until it touches the ground —a good square touch with the ground—the electricians would call it grounded, could I telegraph over that wire? Almost any child knows I could not. Suppose some one cuts the wire, a good clean cut; the two ends are apart: not a mile; not a yard; but distinctly apart. Could I telegraph on that wire? Of course not. Yet I might sit in my room and tick away by the hour wholly absorbed, and use most beautiful persuasive language—what is the good? The wire's cut. All my fine pleading goes into the ground, or the air. Now sin cuts the wire; it runs the message into the ground.

'Well,' someone will object, 'now you're cutting us all out, are you not? Are we not all conscious of a sinful something inside here that has to be fought, and held under all the while?' It certainly seems to be true that the nearer a man gets to God the more keenly conscious he is of a sinful tendency within even while having continual victory. But plainly enough what the Book means here is this:—if I am holding something in my life that the Master does not like, if I am failing to obey when His voice has spoken, that to me is sin. It may be wrong in itself. It may not be wrong in itself. It may not be wrong for another. Sometimes it is not the thing involved but the One involved that makes the issue. If that faithful quiet inner voice has spoken and I know what the Master would prefer and I fail to keep in line, that to me is sin. Then prayer is useless; sheer waste of breath. Aye, worse, it is deceptive. For I am apt to say or think, 'Well, I am not as good as you, or you, but then

I am not so bad; *I pray.*' And the truth is because I have broken with God the praying—saying words in that form—is utterly worthless.

You see, sin is slapping God in the face. It may be polished, cultured sin. Sin seems capable of taking quite a high polish. Or it may be the common gutter stuff. A man is not concerned about the grain of a club that strikes him a blow. How can He and I talk together if I have done that, and stick to it—not even apologized. And of what good is an apology if the offence is being repeated. And if we cannot talk together of course, working together is out of the question. And prayer is working together with God. Prayer is pulling with God in His plan for a world.

Shall we not put out the thing that is wrong? or put in the thing the Master wants in? For Jesus' sake? Aye, for men's sake: poor be-fooled men's sake who are being kept out and away because God cannot get at them through us!

Shall we bow and ask forgiveness for our sin, and petty stubbornness that has been thwarting the Master's love-plan? And yet even while we ask forgiveness there are lives out yonder warped and dwarfed and worse because of the hindrance in us; yes, and remaining so while we read these words. May the fact send us out to walk very softly these coming days.

There is a second thing that is plainly spoken of that hinders prayer. James speaks of it in his letter. (James 4. 2, 3): 'Ye have not because ye *ask* not'—that explains many parched-up lives and churches and unsolved problems: no pipe lines run up to tap the reservoir, and give God an opening into the troubled territory. Then he pushes on to say—'Ye ask, and receive not'—ah! there's just the rub; it is evidently an old story, this thing of not receiving—why?—'because ye ask amiss to spend it in your pleasures.' That is to say selfish praying; asking for something just because I want it; want it for myself.

Here is a mother praying for her boy. He is just growing up towards young manhood; not a Christian boy yet; but a good boy. She is thinking, 'I want *my* boy to be an honour to me; he bears my name; my blood is in his veins; I don't want my boy to be a prodigal. I want him to be a fine man, an honour to the family; and if he is a true Christian, he likely will be; I wish he were a Christian.' And so she prays, and prays repeatedly and fervently. God might touch her boy's heart and say, 'I want you out here in India to help win my prodigal world back.' Oh! she did not mean that! *Her* boy in far, far off India! Oh, no! Not that! Yes, what *she* wanted— that was the whole thought—selfishness; the stream turning in to a dead sea within her own narrow circle; no thought of sympathy with God in His eager outreach for His poor sin-befooled world. The prayer itself in its object is perfectly proper, and rightly offered and answered times without number; but the motive wholly, uglily selfish and the selfishness itself becomes a foothold for Satan and so the purpose of the prayer is thwarted.

Here is a wife praying that her husband might become a Christian. Perhaps her thought is: 'I wish John were a Christian: it would be so good: it really seems the proper thing: he would go to church with me, and sit in the pew Sunday morning: I'd like that.' Perhaps she thinks: 'He would be careful about swearing; he would quit drinking; and be nicer and gentler at home.' Maybe she thinks: 'He would ask a blessing at the meals; that would be so nice.' Maybe she thinks: 'We would have family prayers.' Maybe that does not occur to her these days. This is what I say: If her thought does not go beyond some such range, of course *you* would say it is selfish. She is thinking of herself; not of the loving, grieved God against whom her husband is in rebellion; not of the real significance to the man. God might touch her husband's heart, and then say: 'I want you to help Me win My poor world back.' And the change would mean a reduced income, and a different social position. Oh! she had not meant that! Yes—what *she* wanted for herself!

Here is a minister praying for a revival in his church. Maybe he is thinking; no, not exactly thinking; it is just half thinking itself out in his sub-consciousness—'I wish we had a good revival in our church; increased membership; larger attendance; easier finances; maybe an extra hundred or two in my own pocket; increased prestige in the denomination; a better call or appointment: I wish we might have a revival.' Now no true minister ever talked that way even to himself or deliberately thought it. To do so would be to see the mean contemptibility of it. But you know how sly we all are in our underneath scarcely-thought-out thoughts. This is what I say: if that be the sort of thing underneath a man's praying of course the motive is utterly selfish; a bit of the same thing that brought Satan his change of name and character.

Please notice that the reason for the prayer not being answered here is not an arbitrary reluctance upon God's part to do a desirable thing. He never fails to work whenever He has a half chance as far as it is possible to work, even through men of faulty conceptions and mixed motives. The reason lies much deeper. It is this: selfishness gives Satan a footing. It gives a coaling station for his fleet on the shore of your life. And of course he does his best to prevent the prayer, or when he cannot wholly prevent, to spoil the results as far as he can.

Prayer may properly be offered—will be properly offered for many wholly personal things; for physical strength, healing in sickness, about dearly loved ones, money needed; indeed regarding things that may not be necessary but only desirable and enjoyable, for ours is a loving God who would have His dear ones enjoy to the full their lives down here. But the motive determines the propriety of such requests. Where the whole purpose of one's life is for Him these things may be asked for freely as His gracious Spirit within guides. And there need be no bondage of morbid introspection, no continual internal rakings. He knows if the purpose of the heart is to please Him.

A third thing spoken of as hindering prayer is an unforgiving spirit. You have noticed that Jesus speaks much about prayer and also speaks much about forgiveness. But have you noticed how, over and over again He couples these two—prayer and forgiveness? I used to wonder why. I do not so much now. Nearly everywhere evidence keeps slipping in of the sore spots. One may try to keep his lips closed on certain subjects, but it seems about impossible to keep the ears entirely shut. And continually the evidence keeps sifting in revealing the thin skin, raw flesh, wounds never healed over, and some jaggedly open, almost everywhere one goes. Jesus' continual references reveal how strikingly alike is the oriental and the occidental; the first and the twentieth centuries.

Run through Matthew alone a moment. Here in the fifth chapter: 'If thou art coming to the altar'—that is approaching God; what we call prayer—'and rememberest that thy brother hath aught against thee'—that side of it—'leave there thy gift and go thy way, first be reconciled,' and so on. Here comes a man with a lamb to offer. He approaches solemnly, reverently, towards the altar of God. But as he is coming there flashes across his mind the face of *that man*, with whom he has had difficulty. And instantly he can feel his grip tightening on the offering, and his teeth shutting closer at the quick memory. Jesus says, 'If that be so lay your lamb right down.' What! go abruptly away! Why! How the folks around the temple will talk! 'Lay the lamb right down, and go thy way.' The shortest way to God for that man is not the way to the altar, but around by that man's house. *First*, be reconciled—keep your perspective straight—follow the right order—*first* be reconciled—not second; *then* come and offer thy gift.

In the sixth chapter He gives the form of prayer which we commonly call the Lord's prayer. It contains seven petitions. At the close He stops to emphasize just one of the seven. You remember which one; the one about forgiveness. In the eighteenth chapter Jesus is talking alone with the disciples about prayer. Peter seems to remember the previous remarks about forgiveness in connection with prayer; and he asks a question. It is never difficult to think of Peter asking a question or making a few remarks. He says, 'Master, how many times *must* I forgive a man? Seven times!' Apparently Peter thinks he is growing in grace. He can actually think now of forgiving a man seven times in succession. But the Master in effect says, 'Peter, you haven't caught the idea. Forgiveness is not a question of mathematics; not a matter of keeping tab on somebody: not seven times but seventy times seven.' And Peter's eyes bulge open with an incredulous stare—'four hundred and ninety times! . . . one man—straightway!' Apparently the Master is thinking that he will lose count, or get tired of counting and conclude that forgiveness is preferable,

or else by practice breathe in the spirit of forgiveness—
the thing He meant.

Then as He was so fond of doing Jesus told a story to
illustrate His meaning. A man owed his lord a great
debt, twelve millions of dollars; that is to say practically
an unpayable amount. By comparison with money
to-day, in the western world, it would be about twelve
billions. And he went to him and asked for time. He
said: 'I'm short just now; but I mean to pay; I don't
mean to shirk: be easy with me; and I'll pay up the whole
sum in time.' And his lord generously forgave him the
whole debt. That is Jesus' picture of God, as He knows
Him who knows Him best. Then this forgiven man went
out and found a fellow servant who owed him—how
much do you think? Have you ever thought that Jesus
had a keen sense of the ludicrous? Surely it shows here.
He owed him about sixteen dollars and a quarter or a half!
And you can almost feel the clutch of this fellow's
fingers on the other's throat at he sternly demands:
'Pay me that thou owest.' And his fellow earnestly
replies, 'Please be easy with me; I mean to pay; I'm
rather short just now: but I'm not trying to shirk; be easy
with me.' Is it possible the words do not sound familiar!
But he would not, but put him in the jail. The last place
to pay a debt! That is Jesus' picture of man as He knows
him who knows him best. And in effect He says what
we have been forgiven by God is as an unpayable amount.
And what we are not willing to forgive is like sixteen
dollars and a fraction by contrast. What little puny folks
some of us are in our thinking and feeling!

'Oh, well,' some one says, 'you do not know how hard
it is to forgive.' You think not? I know this much—
that some persons, and some things you *cannot* forgive
of yourself. But I am glad to say that I know this, too,

that if one allows the Spirit of Jesus to sway the heart He will make you love persons you cannot like. No natural affinity or drawing together through disposition, but a real yearning love in the heart. Jesus' love, when allowed to come in as freely as He means, fills your heart with pity for the man who has wounded you. An infinite, tender pity that he has sunk so low as to be capable of such actions.

But the fact to put down in the sharpest contrast of white and black is that we must forgive freely, frankly, generously, 'even as God,' if we are to be in prayer touch with God.

And the reason is not far to find; a double reason, Godward and Satanward. If prayer be partnership in the highest sense then the same spirit must animate both partners, the human and the divine, if the largest results are to come. And since unforgiveness roots itself down in hate Satan has room for both feet in such a heart with all the leeway in action of such purchase. That word *unforgiving*! What a group of relatives it has, near and far! Jealousy, envy, bitterness, the cutting word, the polished shaft of sarcasm with the poisoned tip, the green eye, the acid saliva—what kinsfolk these!

Sin, selfishness, an unforgiving spirit—what searchlights these words are! Many a splendid life to-day is an utter cipher in the spirit atmosphere because of some such hindrance. And God's great love-plan for His prodigal world is being held back; and lives being lost even where ultimately souls shall be saved because of the lack of human prayer partners.

May we not well pray: Search me, O God, and know my heart and help me know it; try me and know my innermost, undermost thoughts and purposes and ambitions, and help me know them; and see what way there be in me that is a grief to Thee; and then lead me—and here the prayer may be a purpose as well as a prayer— lead me out of that way unto Thy way, the way everlasting. For Jesus' sake; aye, for men's sake, too.

PRAYER

WHAT DID THE MASTER DO?

WHEN God would win back His prodigal world He sent down a Man. That Man while more than man insisted upon being truly a man. He touched human life at every point. No man seems to have understood prayer, and to have prayed as did He. Shall we then gather about His person and study His habits of prayer.

A habit is an act repeated so often as to be done involuntarily; that is, without a new decision of the mind each time it is done.

Jesus prayed. He loved to pray. Sometimes praying was His way of resting. He prayed so much and so often that it became a part of His life. It became to Him like breathing—involuntary.

There is no thing we need so much as to learn how to pray. There are two ways of receiving instruction: one, by being told; the other, by watching someone else. The latter is the simpler and the surer way. How better can we learn how to pray than by watching how Jesus prayed, and then trying to imitate Him. Not, just now, studying what He said about prayer, invaluable as that is, and so closely interwoven with the other; nor yet how He received the requests of men when on earth, full of inspiring suggestion as that is of His present attitude towards our prayers; but how He Himself prayed when down here surrounded by our same circumstances and temptations.

There are two sections of the Bible to which we at once turn for light, the gospels and the Psalms. In the gospels is given chiefly the outer side of His prayer-habits; and in certain of the Psalms, glimpses of the inner side are unmistakably revealed.

Turning now to the gospels, we find the picture of the praying Jesus like an etching, a sketch in black and white, the fewest possible strokes of the pen, a scratch here, a line there, frequently a single word added by one writer to the narrative of the others, which gradually bring to view the outline of a lone figure with upturned face.

Of the fifteen mentions of His praying found in the Four Gospels, it is interesting to note that while Matthew gives three, and Mark and John each four, it is Luke, Paul's companion and mirror-like friend, who, in eleven such allusions, supplies most of the picture.

Does this not contain a strong hint of the explanation of that other etching plainly traceable in the epistles which reveals Paul's own marvellous prayer-life?

Matthew, immersed in the Hebrew Scriptures, writes to the Jews of their promised Davidic King; Mark, with rapid pen, relates the ceaseless activity of this wonderful servant of the Father. John, with imprisoned body, but rare liberty of vision, from the glory-side revealed on Patmos, depicts the Son of God coming on an errand from the Father into the world, and again, leaving the world and going back home unto the Father. But Luke emphasizes the human Jesus, a Man—with reverence let me use a word in its old-fashioned meaning—a fellow, that is, one of ourselves. And the Holy Spirit makes it very plain throughout Luke's narrative that the man Christ Jesus prayed; prayed much; needed to pray; loved to pray.

Oh! when shall we men down here, sent into the world as He was sent into the world, with the same mission, the same field, the same Satan to combat, the same Holy

Spirit to empower, find out that power lies in keeping closest connection with the Sender, and completest insulation from the power-absorbing world!

Let me rapidly sketch those fifteen mentions of the Gospel writers, attempting to keep their chronological order.

The first mention is by Luke, in chapter three. The first three Gospels all tell of Jesus' double baptism, but it is Luke who adds, 'and praying.' It was while waiting in prayer that He received the gift of the Holy Spirit. He dared not begin His public mission without that anointing. It had been promised in the prophetic writings. And now, standing in the Jordan, He waits and prays until the blue above is burst through by the gleams of glory-light from the upper-side and the dove-like Spirit wings down and abides upon Him. Prayer brings power. Prayer *is* power. The time of prayer is the time of power. The place of prayer is the place of power. Prayer is tightening the connections with the divine dynamo so that the power may flow freely without loss or interruption.

The second mention is made by Mark in chapter one. Luke, in chapter four, hints at it, 'when it was day He came out and went into a desert place.' But Mark tells us plainly 'in the morning a great while before the day (or a little more literally, "very early while it was yet very dark") He arose and went out into the desert or solitary place and there prayed.' The day before, a Sabbath day spent in His adopted home-town Capernaum, had been a very busy day for Him, teaching in the synagogue service, the interruption by a demon-possessed man, the casting out amid a painful scene; afterwards the healing of Peter's mother-in-law, and then at sun-setting the great crowd of diseased and demonized thronging the narrow street until far into the night, while He, passing amongst them, by personal touch, healed and restored every one. It was a long and exhausting day's work. One of us spending as busy a Sabbath would probably feel that the next morning needed an extra hour's sleep if possible. One must rest surely. But this man Jesus seemed to have another way of resting in addition to sleep. Probably He occupied the guest-chamber in Peter's home. The house was likely astir at the usual hour, and by and by breakfast was ready, but the Master had not appeared yet, so they waited a bit. After a while the maid slips to His room door and taps lightly, but there's no answer; again a little bolder knock, then pushing the door ajar she finds the room unoccupied. Where's the Master? 'Ah!' Peter says, 'I think I know. I have noticed before this that He has a way of slipping off early in the morning to some quiet place where He can be alone.' And a little knot of disciples with Peter in the lead starts out on a search for Him, for already a crowd is gathering at the door and filling the street again, hungry for more. And they 'tracked Him down' here and there on the hillsides, among clumps of trees, until suddenly they come upon Him quietly praying with a wondrous calm in His great eyes. Listen to Peter as he eagerly blurts out, 'Master, there's a big crowd down there, all asking for You.' But the Master's quiet decisive tones reply, 'Let us go into the next towns that I may preach there also; for to this end came I forth.' Much easier to go back and deal again with the old crowd of yesterday; harder to meet the new crowds with their new scepticism, but there's no doubt about what should be done. Prayer wonderfully clears the vision; steadies the nerves; defines duty; stiffens the purpose; sweetens and strengthens the spirit. The busier the day for Him the more surely must the morning appointment be kept, and even an earlier start made, apparently. The more virtue went forth from Him, the more certainly must He spend time, and even more time, alone with Him who is the source of power.

The third mention is in Luke, chapter five. Not a great while after the scene just described, possibly while on the trip suggested by His answer to Peter, in some one of the numerous Galilean villages, moved with the compassion that ever burned in His heart, He had healed a badly diseased leper, who, disregarding His express command, so widely published the fact of His remarkable healing that great crowds blocked Jesus' way in the village and compelled Him to go out to the country district, where the crowds which the village could not hold now throng about Him. Now note what the Master does. The Authorized Version says, 'He withdrew into the wilderness and prayed.' A more nearly literal reading would be, 'He was retiring in the deserts and praying'; suggesting not a single act, but rather a habit of action running through several days or even weeks. That is, being compelled by the greatness of the crowds to go into the deserts or country districts, and being constantly thronged there by the people, He had less opportunity to get alone, and yet there was more need. So while He patiently continues His work among them He studiously seeks opportunity to retire at intervals from the crowds to pray.

How much His life was like ours. Pressed by duties, by opportunities for service, by the great need around us, we are strongly tempted to give less time to the inner chamber, with door shut. 'Surely this work must be done,' we think, 'though it does crowd and flurry our prayer time some.' 'No,' the Master's practice here says with intense emphasis. Not work first, and prayer to bless it. But the first place given to prayer and then the

service growing out of such prayer will be charged with
unmeasured power. The greater the outer pressure on
His closet-life, the more jealously He guarded against
either a shortening of its time or a flurrying of its spirit.
The tighter the tension, the more time must there be for
unhurried prayer.

The fourth mention is found in Luke, chapter six.
'It came to pass in these days that He went out into the
mountains to pray, and He continued all night in prayer
to God.' The time is probably about the middle of the
second year of His public ministry. He had been having
very exasperating experiences with the national leaders
from Judea who dogged His steps, criticising and nagging
at every turn, sowing seeds of scepticism among His
simple-minded, intense-spirited Galileans. It was also
the day before He selected the twelve men who were to
be the leaders after His departure, and preached the
mountain sermon. Luke does not say that He planned
to spend the entire night in prayer. Wearied in spirit by
the ceaseless petty picking and Satanic hatred of His
enemies, thinking of the serious work of the morrow,
there was just one thing for Him to do. He knew where
to find rest, and sweet fellowship, and a calming presence,
and wise counsel. Turning His face northward He
sought the solitude of the mountain not far off for quiet
meditation and prayer. And as He prayed and listened
and talked without words, daylight gradually grew into
twilight, and that yielded imperceptibly to the brilliant
Oriental stars spraying down their lustrous fire-light.
And still He prayed, while the darkness below and the
blue above deepened, and the stilling calm of God
wrapped all nature around, and hushed His heart into a
deeper peace. In the fascination of the Father's loving
presence He was utterly lost to the flight of time, but

prayed on and on until, by and by, the earth had once more completed its daily turn, the grey streaks of dawn-light crept up the east, and the face of Palestine, fragrant with the deep dews of an eastern night, was kissed by a sun of a new day. And then, 'when it was day'—how quietly the narrative goes on—'He called the disciples and chose from them twelve—and a great multitude of disciples and of the people came—and He healed all—and He opened His mouth and taught them—*for power came forth from Him.*' Is it any wonder, after such a night! If all our exasperations and embarrassments were followed and all our decisions and utterances preceded by unhurried prayer, what power would come forth from us, too. Because as He is even so are we in this world.

The fifth mention is made by Matthew, chapter four-teen, and Mark, chapter six, John hinting at it in chapter six of his gospel. It was about the time of the third passover, the beginning of His last year of service. Both He and the disciples had been kept exceedingly busy with the great throng coming and going incessantly. The startling news had just come of the tragic death of His forerunner. There was need of bodily rest, as well as of quiet to think over the rapidly culminating opposition. So taking boat they headed towards the eastern shore of the lake. But the eager crowds watched the direction taken and spreading the news, literally 'ran' around the head of the lake and 'outwent them,' and when He stepped from the boat for the much-needed rest there was an immense company, numbering thousands, waiting for Him. Did some feeling of impatience break out among the disciples that they could not be allowed a little leisure? Very likely, for they were so much like us. But *He* was 'moved with compassion' and, wearied though He was, patiently spent the entire day in teaching, and then, at eventime when the disciples proposed sending them away for food, He, with a handful of loaves and fishes, satisfied the bodily cravings of as many as five thousand.

There is nothing that has so appealed to the masses in all countries and all centuries as ability to furnish plenty to eat. Literally tens of thousands of the human race fall asleep every night hungry. So here. At once it is proposed by a great popular uprising, under the leadership of this wonderful man as king, to throw off the oppressive Roman yoke. Certainly if only His consent could be had it would be immensely successful, they thought. Does this not rank with Satan's suggestion in the wilderness, and with the later possibility coming through the visit of the Greek deputation, of establishing the kingdom without suffering? It was a temptation, even though it found no response within Him. With the over-aweing power of His presence so markedly felt at times, He quieted the movement, 'constrained'* the disciples to go by boat before Him to the other side while He dismissed the throng. 'And after He had taken leave of them'—what gentle courtesy and tenderness mingled with His irrevocable decision—'He went up in the mountain to pray,' and 'continued in prayer' until the morning watch. A second night spent in prayer! Bodily weary, His spirit startled by an event which vividly foreshadowed His own approaching violent death, and now this vigorous renewal of His old temptation, again He had recourse to His one unfailing habit of getting off alone *to pray*. Time alone to pray; more time to pray, was His one invariable offset to all difficulties, all temptations, and all needs. How much more there must have been in prayer as He

---

*Does not this very strong language suggest that possibly the disciples had been conferred with by the revolutionary leaders?

understood and practised it, than many of His disciples
to-day know.

We shall perhaps understand better some of the remaining prayer incidents if we remember that Jesus is
now in the last year of His ministry, the acuge state of His
experiences with the national leaders preceding the final
break. The awful shadow of the Cross grows deeper and
darker across His path. The hatred of the opposition
leader gets constantly intenser. The conditions of
discipleship are more sharply put. The inability of the
crowds, of the disciples, and others to understand Him
grows more marked. Many followers go back. He seeks
to get more time for intercourse with the twelve. He
makes frequent trips to distant points on the border of
the outside, non-Jewish world. The coming scenes and
experiences—the scene on the little hillock outside
the Jerusalem wall—seem never absent from His
thoughts.

The sixth mention is made by Luke, chapter nine.
They are up north in the neighbourhood of the Roman
city of Caesarea Philippi. 'And it came to pass as He
was praying alone, the disciples were with Him.' Alone,
so far as the multitudes are concerned, but seeming to be
drawing these twelve nearer to His inner life. Some of
these later incidents seem to suggest that he was trying
to woo them into something of the same love for the
fascination of secret prayer that He had. How much
they would need to pray in the coming years when He
was gone. Possibly, too, He yearned for a closer fellowship with them. He loved human fellowship, as Peter
and James and John, and Mary and Martha and many
other gentle women well knew. And there is no fellowship among men to be compared with fellowship in
prayer.

> There is a place where spirits blend,
> Where friend holds fellowship with friend,
> A place than all beside more sweet,
> It is the blood-bought mercy-seat.

The seventh mention is in this same ninth chapter of Luke, and records a third night of prayer. Matthew and Mark also tell of the transfiguration scene, but it is Luke who explains that He went up into the mountain to pray, and that it was as He was praying that the fashion of His countenance was altered. Without stopping to study the purpose of this marvellous manifestation of His divine glory to the chosen three at a time when desertion and hatred were so marked, it is enough now to note the significant fact that it was while He was praying that the wondrous change came. Transfigured while praying! And by His side stood one who centuries before on the earth had spent so much time alone with God that the glory-light of that presence transfigured his face, though he was unconscious of it. A shining face caused by contact with God! Shall not we, to whom the Master has said, 'follow Me,' get alone with Him and His blessed Word, so habitually, with open or uncovered face, that is, with eyesight unhindered by prejudice or self-seeking, that mirroring the glory of His face we shall more and more come to bear His very likeness upon our faces? (2 Cor. 3. 18).

> And the face shines bright
> With a glow of light
> From His presence sent
> Whom she loves to meet.

Yes, the face beams bright
With an inner light
As by day so by night,
In shade as in shine,
With a beauty fine,
That she wist not of,
From some source within,
    And above.

Still the face shines bright
With the glory-light
From the mountain height,
Where the resplendent sight
Of His face
Fills her view
And illumines in turn
First the few,
Then the wide race.

The eighth mention is in the tenth chapter of Luke. He
had organized a band of men, sending them out in twos
into the places he expected to visit. They had returned
with a joyful report of the power attending their work;
and standing in their midst, His own heart overflowing
with joy, He looked up and, as though the Father's face
was visible, spake out to Him the gladness of His heart.
He seemed to be always conscious of His Father's presence, and the most natural thing was to speak to Him.
They were always within speaking distance of each other,
and always on speaking terms.

The ninth mention is in the eleventh chapter of Luke,
very similar to the sixth mention, 'It came to pass as He

was praying in a certain place that when He ceased one
of His disciples said unto Him, "Lord, teach us to pray."'
Without doubt these disciples were praying men. He
had already talked to them a great deal about prayer.
But as they noticed how large a place prayer had in His
life, and some of the marvellous results, the fact came
home to them with great force that there must be some
fascination, some power, some secret in prayer, of which
they were ignorant. This Man was a master in the fine
art of prayer. They really did not know how to pray,
they thought. How their request must have delighted
Him! At last they were being aroused concerning the
great secret of power. May it be that this simple recital
of His habits of prayer may move every one of us to get
alone with Him and make the same earnest request.
For the first step in learning to pray is to pray—'Lord,
teach me to pray.' And who can teach like Him?

The tenth mention is found in John, chapter eleven,
and is the second of the four instances of ejaculatory
prayer. A large company is gathered outside the village
of Bethany, around a tomb in which four days before the
body of a young man had been laid away. There is Mary,
still weeping, and Martha, always keenly alive to the
proprieties, trying to be more composed, and their
personal friends, and the villagers, and the company of
acquaintances and others from Jerusalem. At His word,
after some hesitation, the stone at the mouth of the tomb
is rolled aside. And Jesus lifted up His eyes and said,
'Father, I thank Thee that Thou heardest Me; and I
knew that Thou hearest Me always; but because of the
multitude that standeth around I said it that they may
believe that Thou didst send Me!' Clearly before coming
to the tomb He had been praying in secret about the
raising of Lazarus, and what followed was in answer to

His prayer. How plain it becomes that all the marvellous power displayed in His brief earthly career came through prayer. What inseparable intimacy between His life of activity at which the multitude then and ever since has marvelled, and His hidden closet-life of which only these passing glimpses are obtained. Surely the greatest power entrusted to man is prayer-power. But how many of us are untrue to the trust, while this strangely omnipotent power put into our hands lies so largely unused.

Note also the certainty of His faith in the Hearer of prayer: 'I thank Thee that Thou heardest Me.' There was nothing that could be seen to warrant such faith. There lay the dead body. But He trusted as seeing Him who is invisible. Faith is blind, except upward. It is blind to impossibilities and deaf to doubt. It listens only to God and sees only His power and acts accordingly. Faith is not believing that He *can* but that He *will*. But such faith comes only of close continuous contact with God. Its birthplace is in the secret closet; and time and the open Word, and an awakened ear and a reverent quiet heart are necessary to its growth.

The eleventh mention is found in the twelfth chapter of John. Two or three days before the fated Friday some Greek visitors to the Jewish feast of Passover sought an interview with Him. The request seemed to bring to His mind a vision of the great outside world, after which His heart yearned, coming to Him so hungry for what only He could give. And instantly athwart that vision like an ink-black shadow came the other vision, never absent now from His waking thoughts, of the cross so awfully near. Shrinking in horror from the second vision, yet knowing that only through its realization could be realized the first—seemingly forgetful for the moment of the bystanders, as though soliloquizing, He speaks—

'now is My soul troubled; and what shall I say? Shall I say, Father *save* Me from this hour? But for this cause came I unto this hour: *this* is what I will say (and the intense conflict of soul merges into the complete victory of a wholly surrendered will) Father, glorify Thy Name.' Quick as the prayer was uttered, came the audible voice out of heaven answering, 'I have both glorified it and will glorify it again.' How near heaven must be! How quickly the Father hears! He must be bending over, intently listening, eager to catch even faintly whispered prayer. Their ears, full of earth-sounds, unaccustomed to listening to a heavenly voice, could hear nothing intelligible. He had a trained ear. Isaiah 50. 4 revised (a passage plainly prophetic of Him), suggests how it was that He could understand this voice so easily and quickly. 'He wakeneth morning by morning, He wakeneth mine ear to hear as they that are taught.' A taught ear is as necessary to prayer as a taught tongue, and the daily morning appointment with God seems essential to both.

The twelfth mention is made by Luke, chapter twenty-two. It is Thursday night of Passion week, in the large upper room in Jerusalem where He is celebrating the old Passover feast, and initiating the new memorial feast. But even that hallowed hour is disturbed by the disciples' self-seeking disputes. With the great patience of great love He gives them the wonderful example of humility of which John thirteen tells, speaking gently of what it meant, and then turning to Peter, and using his old name, He says, 'Simon, Simon, behold Satan asked to have you that he might sift you as wheat, but I made supplication for thee that thy faith fail not.' He had been praying for Peter by name! That was one of His prayer-habits, praying for others. And He has not broken off that blessed habit yet. He is able to save to the uttermost them that draw near to God through Him seeing He ever liveth to make intercession for them. His occupation now seated at His Father's right hand in glory is praying for each of us who trust Him. By name? Why not?

The thirteenth mention is the familiar one in John, chapter seventeen, and cannot be studied within these narrow limits, but merely fitted into its order. The twelfth chapter contains His last words to the world. In the thirteenth and through to the close of this seventeenth He is alone with His disciples. If this prayer is read carefully in the Revised Version it will be seen that its standpoint is that of one who thinks of His work down in the world as already done (though the chief scene is yet to come) and the world left behind, and now He is about to re-enter His Father's presence to be reinstated in glory there. It is really, therefore, a sort of specimen of the praying for us in which He is now engaged, and so is commonly called the intercessory or high-priestly prayer. For thirty years He lived a perfect life. For three and a half years He was a prophet speaking to men for God. For nineteen centuries He has been high priest speaking to God for men. When He returns it will be as King to reign over men for God.

The fourteenth mention brings us within the sadly sacred precincts of Gethsemane garden, one of His favourite prayer-spots, where He frequently went while in Jerusalem. The record is found in Matthew twenty-six, Mark fourteen, and Luke twenty-one. Let us approach with hearts hushed and heads bared and bowed, for this is indeed hallowed ground. It is a little later on that same Thursday night, into which so much has already been pressed and so much more is yet to come. After the talk in the upper room, and the simple wondrous prayer, He leads the little band out of the city gate on

the east across the swift, muddy Kidron into the enclosed
grove of olive trees beyond. There would be no sleep for
Him that night. Within an hour or two the Roman
soldiers and the Jewish mob, led by the traitor, will be
there searching for Him, and He meant to spend the
intervening time in prayer. With the longing for sympathy so marked during these latter months, He takes
Peter and James and John and goes farther into the
deeply-shadowed grove. But now some invisible power
tears him away and plunges Him alone still farther into
the moonlit recesses of the garden; and there a strange,
awful struggle of soul ensues. It seems like a renewal
of the same conflict He experienced in John twelve when
the Greeks came, but immeasurably intenser. He who
in Himself knew no sin was now beginning to realize in
His spirit what within a few hours He realized *actually*,
that He was in very deed to be made sin for us. And the
awful realization comes in upon Him with such terrific
intensity that it seems as though His physical frame
cannot endure the strain of mental agony. The actual
experience of the next day produced such mental agony
that His physical strength gave way. For He died not of
His physical suffering, excruciating as that was, but literally of a broken heart, its walls burst asunder by the strain
of soul. It is not possible for a sinning soul to appreciate
with what nightmare dread and horror the sinless soul of
Jesus must have approached the coming contact with
the sin of a world. With bated breath and reverent
gaze one follows that lonely figure among the trees; now
kneeling, now falling upon His face, lying prostrate, 'He
prayed that *if* it were possible the hour might pass away
from Him.' One snatch of that prayer reaches our ears:
'Abba, Father, all things are possible unto Thee—*if* it be
possible let this cup pass away from Me; nevertheless,

not as I will, but as Thou wilt.' How long He remained so in prayer we do not know, but so great was the tension of spirit that a messenger from heaven appeared and strengthened Him. Even after that 'being in an agony He prayed more earnestly (literally, more stretched out, more strainedly) and His sweat became as it were great clots of blood falling down upon the ground.' When at length He arises from that season of conflict and prayer, the victory seems to be won, and something of the old-time calm reasserts itself. He goes to the sleeping disciples, and mindful of their coming temptation, admonishes them to pray; then returns to the lonely solitude again for more prayer, but the change in the form of prayer tells of the triumph of soul, 'O My Father, if this cup *cannot* pass away except I drink it, Thy will be done.' The victory is complete. The crisis is past. He yields Himself to that dreaded experience through which alone the Father's loving plan for a dying world can be accomplished. Again He returns to the poor, weak disciples, and back again for another bit of strengthening communion, and then the flickering glare of torches in the distance tells Him that 'the hour is come.' With steady step and a marvellous peace lighting His face He goes out to meet His enemies. He overcame in this greatest crisis of His life by prayer.

The fifteenth mention is the final one. Of the seven sentences which He spake upon the cross, three were prayers. Luke tells us that while the soldiers were driving the nails through His hands and feet and lifting the cross into place, He, thinking even then not of self, but of others, said, 'Father, forgive them, they know not what they do.'

It was as the time of the daily evening sacrifice drew on, near the close of that strange darkness which overcast all nature, after a silence of three hours, that He loudly sobbed out the piercing, heart-rending cry, 'My God, My God, why didst Thou forsake Me?' A little later the triumphant shout proclaimed His work done, and then the very last word was a prayer quietly breathed out, as He yielded up His life, 'Father, into Thy hands I commend My spirit.' And so His expiring breath was vocalized into prayer.

It may be helpful to make the following summary of these allusions.

1. *His times of prayer*: His regular habit seems plainly to have been to devote the early morning hour to communion with His Father, and to depend upon that for constant guidance and instruction. This is suggested especially by Mark 1. 35, and also by Isaiah 50. 4-6 coupled with John 7. 16-18; 8. 28; and 12. 49.

In addition to this regular appointment, He sought other opportunities for secret prayer as special need arose; late at night after others had retired; three times He remained in prayer all the night; and at irregular intervals between times. Note that it was usually a quiet time when the noises of earth were hushed. He spent special time in prayer before important events and also afterwards. (See mentions 1, 2, 3, 4, 5, 10 and 14).

2. *His places of prayer*: He who said, 'Enter into thine inner chamber and when thou hast shut the door, pray to thy Father in secret,' Himself had no fixed inner chamber, during His public career, to make easier the habitual retirement for prayer. Homeless for the three and a half years of ceaseless travelling, His place of prayer was a desert place—the deserts, the mountains, a solitary place. He loved nature. The hilltop back of Nazareth village, the slopes of Olivet, the hillsides overlooking the Galilean lake, were His favourite places. Note that it was always

8

a quiet place, shut away from the discordant sounds of earth.

3. *His constant spirit of prayer*: He was never out of the spirit of prayer. He could be alone in a dense crowd. It has been said that there are sorts of solitude, namely, of time, as early morning, or late at night; solitude of place, as a hilltop, or forest, or a secluded room; and solitude of spirit, as when one surrounded by a crowd may watch them unmoved, or to be lost to all around in his own inner thought. Jesus used all three sorts of solitude for talking with His Father. (See mentions 8, 10, 11 and 15).

4. *He prayed in the great crises of His life*: Five such are mentioned: before the awful battle royal with Satan in the Quarantanian wilderness at the outset; before choosing the twelve leaders of the new movement; at the time of the Galilean uprising; before the final departure from Galilee for Judea and Jerusalem; and in Gethsemane, the greatest crisis of all. (See mentions 1, 4, 5, 7 and 14).

5. *He prayed for others by name*, and still does. (See mention 13).

6. *He prayed with others*: A habit that might well be more widely copied. A few minutes spent in quiet prayer by friends or fellow-workers before parting wonderfully sweetens the spirit, and cements friendships, and makes difficulties less difficult, and hard problems easier of solution. (See mentions 7, 9 and 13).

7. *The greatest blessings of His life came during prayer*: Six incidents are noted: while praying the Holy Spirit came upon Him; He was transfigured; three times a heavenly voice of approval came; and in His hour of sorest distress in the garden a heavenly messenger came to strengthen Him. (See mentions 1, 7, 11 and 14).

How much prayer meant to Jesus! It was not only His regular habit, but His resort in every emergency, however slight or serious. When perplexed He prayed. When hard pressed by work He prayed. When hungry for fellowship He found it in prayer. He chose His associates and received His messages upon His knees. If tempted, He prayed. If criticised, He prayed. If fatigued in body or wearied in spirit, He had recourse to His one unfailing habit of prayer. Prayer brought Him unmeasured power at the beginning, and kept the flow unbroken and un-diminished. There was no emergency, no difficulty, no necessity, no temptation that would not yield to prayer, as He practised it. Shall not we, who have been tracing these steps in His prayer life, go back over them again and again until we breathe in His very spirit of prayer? And shall we not, too, ask Him daily to teach us how to pray, and then plan to get alone with Him regularly that He may have opportunity to teach us, and we the oppor-tunity to practise His teaching?

> Lord, what a change within us one short hour
>
> Spent in Thy presence will prevail to make—
>
> What heavy burdens from our bosoms take,
>
> What parchèd grounds refresh as with a shower!
>
> We kneel and all around us seems to lower;
>
> We rise, and all, the distant and the near,
>
> Stands forth in sunny outline, brave and clear;
>
> We kneel how weak, we rise how full of power!
>
> Why, therefore, should we do ourselves this wrong,
>
> Or others—that we are not always strong;
>
> That we are ever overborne with care;

That we should ever weak or heartless be,
Anxious or troubled, when with us is prayer,
And joy and strength and courage are with thee?

Trench

POWER

My power is faint and low
   Till I have learned to serve:
It wants the needed fire to glow,
   It wants the breeze to nerve;
It cannot drive the world
   Until itself be driven;
Its flag can only be unfurled
   When Thou shalt breathe from heaven.

G. Matheson

distinctly his reply, after a moment's pause: 'Well, their condition certainly will be unfortunate.' *Unfortunate*! That is the Bostonese of it. That is a much less disagreeable word. It has a smoother finish—a sort of polish —to it. It does not jar on your feelings so. But this Book uses a very different word from that, a word that must grate harshly upon every ear here.

I know very well that some persons have associated that ugly word with a scene something like this: They have imagined a man standing with fist clenched, and eyes flashing fire, and the lines of his face knotted up hard, as he says in a harsh voice, 'He that believeth not shall be damned,' as though he found pleasure in saying it. If there is *one* person reading this who ever had such a conception, will you kindly cut it out of your imagination at once? For it is untrue. And put in its place the true setting of the word.

Have you ever noticed what a difference the manner, and expression of face, and tone of voice, yes, and the character of a person, make in the impression his words leave upon your mind? Now, mark: It is Jesus talking here. *Jesus*—the tenderest-hearted, the most mother-hearted man this world ever listened to. Look at Him standing there on that hilltop, looking out toward the great world He had just died for, with the tears coming into His eyes, and His lips quivering with the awfulness of what He was saying—'he that believeth not shall be damned,' as though it just broke His heart to say it. And it did break His heart that it might not be true of us. For He died literally of a broken heart, the walls of that great throbbing muscle burst asunder by the strain of soul. That is the true setting of that terrific statement.

Please notice it does not say that God damns men. You will find that nowhere within the pages of the Bible.

But it is love talking. And true love tells the truth at all risks when it must be told. And Jesus because of His dying and undying love seeks to make men acquainted with the fact which *He* sees so plainly, and *they* do not.

Now think for a moment of a second statement. You will find it in Galatians, third chapter, tenth verse. Paul is quoting from the book of Deuteronomy these words: 'Cursed'—there is another ugly word—'cursed is everyone who continueth not in all the words of the book of this law to do them.' Let me ask: Does that describe your friends? Well, I guess it describes us all, does it not? Who is there here that has continued in all the words of the book of this law to do them? If there is someone I think perhaps you would better withdraw, for I have no message for you. The sole difference between some of us, and these friends you have in your mind is that *we* are depending upon Another who bore the curse for us. But these friends decline to come into personal touch with Him. Do they not? And this honest spoken Book of God tells us plainly of that word 'cursed' which has been written, and remains written, over their faces and lives.

The Bible is full of such statements. There is no need of multiplying them. And I am sure I have no heart in repeating any more of them. But I bring you these two for a purpose. This purpose: of asking you one question —whose fault is it? Who is to blame? Someone is at fault. There is blame somewhere. This thing is all wrong. It is no part of God's plan, and when things go wrong, someone is to blame. Now I ask you: *Who* is to blame?

Well, there are just four persons and groups of persons concerned. There is God; and Satan; and these friends we are talking about; and, ourselves, who are not a bit better in ourselves than they—not a bit—but who are trusting Someone else to see us through. Somewhere within the lines of those four we must find the blame of this awful state of affairs. Well, we can say very promptly that Satan is to blame. He is at the bottom of it all. And that certainly is true, though it is not all of the truth. Then it can be added, and added in a softer voice, because the thing is so serious, and these things are dear to us, that these people themselves are to blame. And that is true, too. Because they *choose* to remain out of touch with Him who died that it might not be so. For there is no sin charged where there is no choice made. Sin follows choice. Only where one has known the wrong and has chosen it is there sin charged.

But that this awful condition goes on unchanged, that those two ugly words remain true of our dear friends, day after day, while we meet them, and live with them, is there still blame? There are just two left out of the four: God and ourselves who trust Him. Let me ask very reverently, but very plainly: Is it God's fault? You and I have both heard such a thing hinted at, and sometimes openly said. I believe it is a good thing with reverence to ask, and attempt to find the answer, to such a question as that. And for answer let me first bring to you a picture of the God of the Old Testament whom some people think of as being just, but severe and stern.

Away back in the earliest time, in the oldest book, Genesis, the sixth chapter, and down in verses five and six are these words: 'And the Lord saw that the wickedness of man was great in the earth, and'—listen to these words—'that every imagination of the thoughts of his heart was only evil continually.'

What an arraignment! Every imagination, evil, *only* evil; no mixture of good at all; only evil *continually*, no occasional spurts of good even—the whole fabric bad, and bad clear through, and all the time. Is not that a terrific arraignment? But listen further: 'And it repented the Lord that He had made man on the earth, and'—listen to these last pathetic words—'*it grieved Him at His heart.*'

Will you please remember that grieve is always a love word? There can be no grief except where there is love. You may annoy a neighbour, or vex a partner, or anger an acquaintance, but you cannot grieve except where there is love, and you cannot be grieved except wherein you love.

I have sometimes, more often than I could wish, seen a case like this. A young man of good family sent away to college. He gets in with the wrong crowd, for they are not all angels in colleges yet, quite. Gets to smoking and drinking and gambling, improper hours, bad companions, and all that. His real friends try to advise him, but without effect. By and by the college authorities remonstrate with him, and he tries to improve, but without much success after the first pull. And after a while, very reluctantly, he is suspended, and sent home in disgrace. He feels very bad, and makes good resolutions and earnest promises, and when he returns he does do much better for a time. But it does not last long. Soon he is in with the old crowd again, the old round of habits and dissipations, only now it gets worse than before; the pace is faster. And the upshot of it all is that he is called up before the authorities and expelled, sent home in utter disgrace, not to return.

And here is his chum who roomed with him, ate with him, lived with him. He says, 'Well, I declare, I am all broken up over Jim. It's too bad! He was a fine fellow, good student, if he only would study; genial, hale fellow well met, and he now has gone to the dogs like that. I'm awfully sorry. It's too bad! too bad!' And by and by he forgets about it except as an unpleasant memory roused up now and then. And here is one of his professors who knew him best perhaps, and liked him. 'Well,' he says, 'it is too bad about young Collins; he was an able fellow, but he would insist on going with that crowd. Strange, too, he came of good family; good blood in his veins; and yet he seems to have gone right down with the rag-tag. It's too bad! too bad! I am so sorry.' And the matter passes from his mind in the press of duties and is remembered only occasionally as one of the disagreeable things to be regretted and perhaps philosophised over.

And there is the boy's father's partner, down in the home town. 'Well,' he soliloquises, 'it is too bad about Collins' boy. He is all broken up over it, and no wonder. Doesn't it seem queer? That boy has as good blood as there is: good father, lovely mother, and yet gone clean to the bad, and so young. It is too bad! I am awfully sorry for Collins.' And he forgets, save as a bad dream which will come back now and then.

But down in that boy's home there is a woman—a mother—heart-broken—crying her eyes out. She goes quietly, faithfully about her round of life, but her hair gets thinner, and the grey streaks it plainer, her form bends over more, and the lines become more deeply bitten in her face, as the days come and go. 'Oh, yes,' she says, 'I know other mothers' boys go wrong; some of them going wrong all the time; but to think of *my Jim*— that I've nursed, and loved so, and done everything for— to think that my Jim——' and her voice chokes in her throat, and she refuses to be comforted. She grieves at her heart. Ah! that is the picture of God in that Genesis chapter. He saw that the world He had made and lavished all the wealth of His love upon had gone wrong, and it grieved Him at His heart. This world is God's prodigal son, and He is heartbroken over it. And what has He done about it? Ah! what has He done! Turn to Mark's twelfth chapter and see there Jesus' own picture of His Father as He knew Him. In the form of a parable He tells how His Father felt about things here. He sent man after man to try and win us back, but without effect, except that things got worse. Then Jesus represents God talking with Himself. 'What *shall* I do next, to win them back?—there is My Son—My only Boy Jesus—I believe—yes, I believe I'll send Him—then they'll *see* how badly I feel, and how much I love them; that'll touch them surely; I'll do it.' You remember just how that sixth verse goes, 'He had yet one, a beloved Son; He sent Him *last* unto them, saying, they will *reverence* My Son.' And you know how they treated God's Son, His love-gift. And I want to remind you to-night that, speaking in our human way—the only way we can speak—God suffered more in seeing His Son suffer than though He might have suffered Himself. Ask any mother: Would you not gladly suffer pain in place of your child suffering if you could? And every mother-heart answers quickly, 'Aye, ten times over, if the child could be spared.' Where did you get that marvellous mother-heart and mother-love? Ah, that mother-heart is a bit of the God-heart. That is what God is like. Let me repeat very reverently that God suffered more in giving His Son to suffer than though He had Himself suffered. And that is the God of the Old Testament! Let me ask: 'Is *He* to blame? Has He not done His best?

Let it be said as softly as you will, and yet very plainly, that those awful words damned and cursed, whatever their

meaning may be, are true of your friends. Then add:
It is not so because of God's will in the matter, but in
spite of His will. Remember that God exhausted all
the wealth of His resource when He gave His Son. There
can come nothing more after that.

Then there is a second question from God's side to ask
about those ugly words: thoughtfully, and yet plainly—
Is it the fault of Jesus, the Son of God? And let anyone
here listen to Him speaking in that tenth chapter of
John. 'I lay down My life for the sheep. No man taketh
it from Me. I lay it down of Myself. I have power to
lay it down and power to take it again.' And then go
out yonder to that scene just outside the Jerusalem wall.
There hangs Jesus upon that Cross, suspended by nails
through hands and feet. He is only thirty-three. He is
intensely human. Life was just as sweet to Him that day
as it is to you and me now. Plainly He could have pre-
vented them. For many a time had He held the murderous
mob in check by the sheer power of His presence alone.
Yet there He hangs from nine until noon and until three
—six long hours. And He said He did it for you, for me.
Do not ask me to tell *how* His dying for us saves. I do
not know. No one statement seems to tell all the truth.
When I study into it I always get clear beyond my depth.
In a tremendous way it tells a double story: of the damn-
able blackness of sin; and of the intensity of love. I
do know that He said He did it for us, and for our salva-
tion, and that it had to be done. But as we look to-day
on that scene, again the question: does any of the blame
of the awful statements this book makes regarding your
friends belong to Him, do you think? And I think I hear
your hearts say, 'surely not.'

Well, the Father has done His best. No blame surely
attaches there. The Son has gone to the utmost limit.

No fault can be found there. There is just one other left up yonder, of the divine partnership—the Holy Spirit. What about Him. Listen. Just as soon as the Son went back home with face and form all scarred from His brief stay upon the earth, He and the Father said, 'now We will send down the last one of Us, the Holy Spirit, and He will do His best to woo men back,' and so it was done. The last supreme effort to win men back was begun. The Holy Spirit came down for the specific purpose of telling the world about Jesus. His work down here is to convict men of their terrible wrong in rejecting Jesus, and of His righteousness, and of the judgment passed upon Satan. Only He can convince men's minds and consciences. A thousand preachers with the logic of a Paul and the eloquence of an Isaiah could not convince one man of sin. Only the Spirit can do that. But listen to me as I say very thoughtfully—and this is the one tremendous truth I pray God to burn into our hearts now—that to do His work among men *He* needs to use men. He needs *you*. 'Oh!' you say, 'it is hardly possible that you mean that; I am not a minister; I have no special ability for Christian work; I am just an obscure, humble Christian; I have no gift in that direction.' Listen with your heart while I remind you that He needs not your special abilities or gifts so much as He needs your personality as a human channel through which to touch the men you touch. And I want to say just as kindly and tenderly as I can and yet with great plainness that if you are refusing to let Him use you as He chooses —shall I say the unpleasant truth?—the practical blame for those ugly words, and the uglier truth back of them come straight home to *you*.

That is a very serious thing to say, and so I must add a few words to make it still more clear and plain. The

Spirit of God in working among men seeks embodiment *in men*, through whom He acts. The amazing truth is that not only is He willing to enter into and fill you with His very presence, but He seeks for, He wants, yes, He needs your personality as a channel or medium, that living in you He may be able to do His work among the men you touch even though you may not be conscious of much that He is doing through you. Is not that startling? He wants to live in your body, and speak through your lips, and look out of your eyes, and use your hands, really, actually. Have you turned your personality over to Him as completely as that?

Remember the law of God's communication with men; namely, He speaks *to* men *through* men. Run carefully through the Bible and you will find that after the Cain disaster, which divided all men into two great groups, that whenever God has a message for a man or a nation out in the world He chooses and uses a man in touch with Himself as His messenger.

Listen to Jesus' own words in that last night's long talk in John's Gospel, chapter fourteen, verse seventeen. Speaking about the coming Spirit, He says, 'Whom the world cannot receive.' Though an important part of the Spirit's great mission is to the world yet it cannot receive Him. Couple that with chapter sixteen, verses seven and eight: 'I will send Him *unto you*, and He when He is come (unto you) will convince,' and so on. That is to say, a message from God to one who has come within the circle of personal relation with Jesus—that message comes along a straight line without break or crook. But a message to one who remains outside that circle comes along an angled line—two lines meeting at an angle— and the point of that angle is in some Christian heart. The message He sends out to the outer circle passes through some one within the inner circle. To make it direct and personal: He needs to use you to touch those whom you touch.

Let me bring you a few illustrations of how God uses men, though the fact of His using them is on almost every page of this Bible. Back in the old Book of Judges is a peculiar expression which is not brought out as clearly as it might be in our Bible. The sixth chapter and thirty-fourth verse should read: 'the Spirit of Jehovah clothed Himself with Gideon.' It was a time of desperate crisis in the nation. God chose this man for leadership among his fellows. If you take his life throughout you will not think him an ideal character. But he seems to be the best available stuff there was. He became the general guiding an army in what to human eyes was a perfectly hopeless struggle. Men saw Gideon moving about giving orders. But this strangely significant phrase lets us into the secret of his wise strategy and splendid victory. 'The Spirit of Jehovah clothed Himself with Gideon.' Gideon's personality was merely a suit of clothes which God wore that day in achieving that tremendous victory for His people. The same expression is used of Amasai, one of David's mighty chieftains, and of Zechariah, one of the priests during Joash's reign.

A New Testament illustration is found in the book of Acts in the account of Philip and the Ethiopian stranger. This devout African official had a copy of the old Hebrew Scriptures, but needed an interpreter to make plain their newly acquired significance. The Holy Spirit, *the* interpreter of Scripture, longs to help him. For that purpose He seeks out a man, of whom He has control, named Philip. He is directed to go some distance over toward the road where this man is journeying. We are told of Philip that he was 'full of the Spirit.' And a reading of that eighth chapter makes plain the controlling presence of the Spirit in Philip's personality. In the beginning He gives very explicit direction. 'The Spirit (within Philip) said, go near, join thyself to this chariot.' And at the close 'the Spirit of the Lord caught away Philip.'

These are a few illustrations of what seems to be a common law of God's intercourse with men. The language of the Bible throughout fits in with this same conception. Strikingly enough the same seems to be true in the opposing camp, among the forces of the Evil One. Repeatedly in the Gospels we come across the startling expressions—'possessed with demons,' 'possessed of demons,' evidently speaking of men whom demons had succeeded in getting possession of, and clothing themselves with. It seems to be a law of *spirit* life that a spirit needs to be embodied in dealing with embodied beings. And God conforms to this law in His dealings with men.

My friend, will you ask your heart, has the Holy Spirit got possession of you like that? With reverence I repeat that He is seeking for men in whom He may set up, a sort of sub-headquarters, from which He may work out as He pleases. Has He been able to do that with you? Or, have you been holding back from Him, fearing He might make some changes in you or your plans? If that is so, may I say just as kindly as these lips can speak it, but also as plainly, that then *the practical blame* for those cutting words about your friends comes straight back to *you*.

Hugh M'Allister Beaver, son of the former Governor of Pennsylvania, and one of the rarest Christian young men that ever lived, felt impelled at a conference of students at Northfield in '97 to tell this bit of his inner experience, though naturally reluctant to do so. While at college, arrangements were made for a series of meetings every night for a week. 'One day going down the hall-way of the college building,' he said, 'I met a boy we all called Dutchy, one of the toughest fellows in school. I said to him, "Dutch, come to the meeting to-night."' Instead of laughing or swearing, to Beaver's surprise, he paused a moment as though such a thing was possible, and Beaver said, 'I prayed quietly to myself, and urged him to come.' And he said, 'Well, I guess I will.' And that night to every one's surprise Dutch came to the meeting. When Beaver rose to speak to his surprise this fellow was not simply intensely interested but his eyes were full of tears. And Beaver said, 'a voice as distinct as an audible voice said to me, "Speak to Dutchy!" But *I did not.*' Again the next night Dutchy came of his own accord, and one of the boys putting his arm on Beaver's shoulder said, 'Speak to Dutchy. We boys never saw him like this before.' And he said he would. But *he did not.* And some time after he had a dream and thought he would not walk this earth any more. It did not trouble him except that his brother was crying. But he thought he met the Master, who looked into his face, and said, 'Hugh, do you remember I asked you to speak to Dutchy?' 'Yes.' 'And you did not.' 'No.' 'Would you like to go back to the earth and win him?' And he finished the story by saying, 'it's hard work, but he's coming now.'

I wonder if the Master has ever tried to use your lips like that, and you have refused?

A prominent clergyman in New England tells this experience of his. In the course of his pastoral work he was called to conduct the funeral service of a young woman who had died quite unexpectedly. As he entered the house he met the minister in charge of the mission church, where the family attended, and asked him, 'Was

Mary a Christian?' To his surprise a pained look came into the young man's face as he replied, 'Three weeks ago I had a strong impulse to speak to her, but *I did not*; and I do not know.' A moment later he met the girl's Sunday School teacher and asked her the same question. Quickly the tears came, as she said, 'Two weeks ago, Doctor, a voice seemed to say to me, "Speak to Mary," and I knew what it meant, and I intended to, but *I did not*, and I do not know.' Deeply moved by these unexpected answers, a few minutes later he met the girl's mother, and thinking doubtless to give her an opportunity to speak a word that would bring comfort to her own heart, he said quietly, 'Mary was a Christian girl?' The tears came quick and hot to the mother's eyes as she sobbed out, 'One week ago a voice came to me saying, "Speak to Mary," and I thought of it, but I did not at the time, and you know how unexpectedly she went away and I do not know.'

Well, please understand me, I am not saying a word about that girl. I do not know anything to say. I would hope much. And believe there was ground for hope. But this is what I say: How pathetic, beyond expression, that the Spirit tried to get the use of the lips of three persons, a pastor, a teacher, aye *a mother*! to speak the word that evidently He longed to have spoken to her, *and He could not*!

Has He tried to use you *like that*?

But these two illustrations are narrower than the truth. They speak of the lips. He wants to use your lips; but, even more, He wants to use your *life*. Much as He may use your lips, He will use your personality, your presence, your life ten times more, when you are wholly unconscious of it. He loves men so much. He longs to save them. But He needs us—you and me—as channels through

which His power shall flow to touch and mightily influence those whom we touch. How often has He turned
away disappointed because the channel had broken
connections, or could not be used?

> He was not willing that any should perish;
>   Jesus, enthroned in the glory above,
> Saw our poor fallen world, pitied our sorrows,
>   Poured out His life for us, wonderful love.
> Perishing, perishing, thronging our pathway,
>   Hearts break with burdens too heavy to bear;
> Jesus would save, but there's no one to tell them,
>   No one to save them from sin and despair.

Someone says: 'You are putting an awful responsibility
upon us. Would you have us go out and begin speaking
to everyone we meet?' No, I would not. Of all things,
I do not mean that. But this: Surrender yourself to Jesus
as your Master, for Him to take possession. Turn the
channel over to Him, that He may tighten the connections
upward and outward, and clean it out, and then use as
He may choose. He has a passion for winning men, and
He has marvellous tact in working. Let Him have His
way in you. Keep quiet and close to Him, and obey
Him, gladly, cheerily, constantly, and *He will assume all
responsibility for the results*.

There is a law of personal service. It is this: Contact
means opportunity; opportunity means responsibility.
To come into personal contact with a man gives an
opportunity of influencing him for Christ, and with
opportunity goes its twin partner—responsibility.

There is another law—a higher law—the highest
law of the Christian life. It is this: In everything hold
yourself subject to the Holy Spirit's leading. Whenever
these two laws come into conflict remember that the

lower law always yields to the higher. It is a law of life that where two laws come into conflict the lower law always gives way to the higher. That is a supreme law both of nature and in legislation. The highest law of the Christian life is to yield constantly to the leading of our Companion—the Holy Spirit. Then quiet time alone with the Master daily over His word for the training of the ear, and the training of the judgment, and the training of the tongue becomes the great essential.

But now the great question is: Have you turned the channel of power—your personality—over to Him to be flushed and flooded with His power? Will you?

> Only a smile, yes, only a smile,
> That woman o'er burdened with grief
> Expected from you; 'twould have given relief,
>   For her heart ached sore the while.
> But weary and cheerless, she went away,
> Because, as it happened that very day,
>   You were out of touch with your Lord.
>
> Only a word, yes, only a word,
> That the Spirit's small voice whispered "Speak";
> But the worker passed onward, unblessed and weak,
>   Whom you were meant to have stirred
> To courage, devotion and love anew,
> Because, when the message came to you,
>   You were out of touch with your Lord.
>
> Only a note, yes, only a note,
> To a friend in a distant land;
> The Spirit said "Write," but then you had planned
>   Some different work, and you thought
> It mattered little. You did not know
> 'Twould have saved a soul from sin and woe—
>   You were out of touch with your Lord.

Only a song, yes, only a song,
That the Spirit said, "Sing to-night;
Thy voice is thy Master's by purchased right."
But you thought, "Mid this motley throng,
I care not to sing of the City of God":
And the heart that your words might have reached
grew cold—
You were out of touch with your Lord.

Only a day, yes, only a day,
But, oh! can you guess, my friend,
Where the influence reaches and where it will end
Of the hours that you frittered away?
The Master's command is, "Abide in Me";
And fruitless and vain will your service be
If out of touch with your Lord.

POWER

WHAT DOES IT COST?

EVERY man needs power. Every earnest man covets power. Every willing man has the Master's promise of power. But every man does not possess the promised power. And many, it is to be feared, never will. Many a man's life to-day is utterly lacking in power. Some of us will look back at the close of life with a sense of keen disappointment and of bitter defeat. And the reason is not far to seek nor hard to see through. If we do not have power it is because we are not willing to pay the price.

Everything costs. There is a law of exchange that rules in every sphere of life. It is this, to get you must give. It rules in the business world. If I want a house or a hat I must give the sum agreed upon. It rules in the intellectual world. If a young man wants a disciplined mind he must give time, and close application, and some real hard work. It holds true in the spirit realm. If you and I wish to have business transactions in this upper world of spirit-life we must be governed by this same law. To have power in our lives over sin and selfishness, and passion, and appetite; over tongue, and temper, and self-seeking ambition; to have power in prayer, and in winning others over from sin to Jesus Christ, one must first lay down the required price.

What is the price of power? Turn to Jesus' talk with Peter and the others in the latter part of the sixteenth chapter of Matthew's Gospel. Jesus has been telling them of the awful Cross experiences which He clearly saw ahead. Peter probably fearful that whatever came to his Master might possibly come to himself also, and shrinking back in horror from that, has the hardihood to rebuke Jesus. The Master, recognizing the suggestion as coming from a far subtler individual than Peter, who is using ignorant Peter's selfishness to repeat the suggestion of the wilderness, again bids *him* begone. Then in a few simple words of far-reaching significance, He states first the standard of power, and then the price to be paid by one who would reach that standard. Listen to Him: 'If any man would come after Me, let him deny himself and take up his cross and follow Me.'

Let us look a little into these familiar words: 'If any man *would come after Me*'—that is the standard set before us. Not to be regarded as a pillar in the church, a leader in religious circles, a good Bible student, a generous worker, an earnest speaker, an energetic worker, a spiritually-minded person, but, what may not be coupled with any or all of these admirable things, *to tread in the footprints of Jesus*.

Think back into that marvellous life. A human life, remember. For though He was Son of God He lived His life down here as a Son of Man. Think of His power over temptation, not alone at the outset in the fierce wilderness struggle, but through those succeeding years of intense conflict; His power over Satan, over man-possessing demons, over disease; His power in dealing with the subtle schoolmen trying their best to trip Him up, as well as over His more violent enemies who would have dashed Him over yon Nazareth precipice, or later stoned the life out of His body in Jerusalem. Recall the power of His rare unselfishness; His combined plainness and tenderness of speech in dealing with men; His unfailing love to all classes; His power as a soul-winner, as a man of prayer, as a popular preacher, lovingly wooing men while unsparingly rebuking their sins. *There* is the suggestion of Jesus' standard of power. Would you go *after Him*? You may. For as the Father sent Him even so sends He us, to do the same work and live the same life.

But wait a moment before answering that question. There is another side in His life to that Come-after-Me. Opposites brought into contact produce a violent disturbance. Such a life as that of Jesus, down in the atmosphere of this world, will of necessity provoke bitter enmities, both then and now. Listen. He was criticised and slandered. They said He was peculiar and fanatical. His friends thought Him beside Himself, swept off His feet by excessive, hot-headed enthusiasm. They laughed Him to scorn, and reviled Him. They picked His words and nagged His kindliest acts, and dogged His steps. Repeated attempts were made upon His life, both at Nazareth and by stoning at Jerusalem. A determined conspiracy against His life was planned by the Jerusalem officials six months before the end actually came. He was practically a fugitive for those months. At the last He was arrested and mocked and spit upon, struck with open hand and clenched fist, derisively crowned with thorns, and finally killed—a cruel, lingering, tortured death.

'If any man would *come after Me*.' Plainly this language of Jesus put back into its original setting begins to assume a new significance.

But look at these words a little more closely. '*If*'—it is an open question, this matter of following Jesus. It is kept open by many people who want to be known as Christian, but who hesitate over what a plain understanding of Jesus' words may involve. Some of us may be disposed to shrink back from the simple meaning these words will yet disclose.

'If any man *would*'—would is the past tense of will. The word will is one of the strongest in our language. A man's will is the imperial part of him. It is the auto-crat upon the throne; the judge upon the bench of final appeal. Jesus is getting down to the root of matters here. He is appealing to the highest authority. No mere passing sentiment is this. Not attending a meeting and being swept along with the crowd by the hour's influence. But a fixed purpose, calmly, resolutely settled upon, rooted away down deep in the very vitals of the will to follow Jesus absolutely, no matter what it may cost or where it may cut.

I wonder how many of us would form such a purpose, to follow Jesus *blindly*, utterly regardless of what it might be found to mean as the days come and go? 'Oh, well,' I hear someone say, 'why talk like that. Nobody is re-quired to suffer to-day as He did.' Do you think not? I am not so sure about that. There is a young man in Southern India, a bright fellow, full of power, of high-class family, who heard of Jesus, and felt the personal appeal to himself of that marvellous story. He thought a good while of what it meant, and what it might involve, and at length resolutely formed his decision to accept and follow Jesus. As he had anticipated, his dear ones remonstrated with him, coaxed, pleaded, threatened, and finally, his own father violently put him out of his life-long home, and he has remained since an outcast from home and loved ones. These words of Jesus surely are full of significance to him.

'But that was in India, far off, heathen India,' you say. Well, here is something of a similar sort at home. I knew a young woman in a certain New England town visiting away from home. She attended some meetings where she was visiting, and decided to be a Christian.

She was betrothed to a young man, not a Christian, in her home town. At once she wrote him explaining her new step thinking doubtless how glad he would be. For most men seem very willing to have their wives Christian. But he wrote back that if she were determined to be a Christian that must put an end to their engagement! He was not a Christian and did not want his wife to be one. Every one here must know how serious a question that brought up for decision. For she was a true woman, and love's tendrils twine with wondrous tenacity about a woman's heart. And I presume, too, that everyone of you has already thought while reading of the temptation that, quick as a flash, went through her mind. 'You need not make a public matter of this. Just be a true Christian in heart and life, and in that way you'll win him over afterwards.' I imagine some of you have heard something like that before. But she remembered that her new Master said confess as well as believe. It was a crisis; a severe struggle of soul. But she felt she must follow her Master's leading regardless of what it involved. And so she decided. You are not surprised to know that she was ill for a time. The intense strain of spirit affected her body. 'If—any—man—would—come—after—Me' meant much to her. Did it not?

Without doubt if some of us listening to-day were to follow Jesus quietly, but absolutely, in all things as His own spirit plainly led, we would find as sharp a line of separation drawn against us, as did He in Palestine, and these young people in India and America.

Many a social door would be shut in our faces. O, shut politely, of course! Society thinks it in very bad form to get unduly excited about mere matters of religious opinion. But the door is shut, and barred, too. Some of us would possibly be searching for other business positions before to-morrow's light faded away if we were determined to go only where *He* clearly pointed the way.

But we have only begun to get at the meaning of Jesus' words. Is there still a fixed purpose to follow regardless of what meaning these words may yet disclose? Not impossibly the company of those willing to go straight through this verse with a calm, determined yes to every word of Jesus, will grow smaller as we go on.

Let us go a little farther. 'If any man would come after Me let him deny himself.' Deny himself—what does that mean? Well, deny means to say 'no,' plainly and positively. Himself is the smoother English word for his-self. Let him say no to his-self. Please notice that Jesus is not speaking of what is commonly called self-denial. That is, representing some desire for a time, sacrificing something temporarily in order to gain an advantage later. That sort of thing is not peculiar to the Christian life, but is practised by all classes, even among the lowest. He is not speaking of that, but something far more radical. Reading the verse through again it will be seen that there are three distinct persons referred to by Jesus. First, the 'any man' He speaks of, and then the two others represented by these words himself and Me, either one or the other of whom is influencing this any man's life. 'Say no to his-self' is coupled with 'follow Me.' And the opposite is implied—'if any man will not do as *I* desire, he will continue to do as he is now doing, namely, 'deny Me and follow his-self.'

These two persons, self and Jesus, are placed here in sharpest contrast. An uncompromising antagonism exists between them. They are sworn foes, and every man must decide to which he will yield his allegiance To agree with either one is to oppose the other one. For a man to settle some matter that comes up for decision by saying yes to the desires or demands of his-self involves his saying no to Jesus. And, on the other hand, his yielding assent to the plans and wishes of this Me, that is, Jesus, is plainly equivalent to saying no to his-self.

What is this self in each of us that Jesus sets in such antagonism to Himself, and instructs us to say a hard, uncompromising, unceasing no to? There are a few words in common use that give some suggestion of its character. There is the word selfish, that is, being absorbed in one's own self; in getting every stream to flow by his own door. That is commonly regarded, even in absolutely worldly circles, as a detestable trait. Its opposite, self-forgetful, forgetting one's self in thinking of others, is as commonly regarded in all circles as a charming, winsome trait of character. The words self-centred, and self-willed, are as familiar and suggestive.

The fact is, there is an individual living inside each one of us whom Jesus refers to, by this word 'his-self.' This individual takes on the degree of intensity and other local colouring of the person it inhabits. It may be polished, scholarly, cultured; or, coarse, ignorant, and ill-mannered. But—scratch a Russian and you find a Tartar. Scratch through the veneering here, and, whether coarse or highly polished, you will find the same individual—self.

There are some quite marked characteristics by which its presence may be recognized. They may not all be noticeable together in any one person. But one or more will be found in every person whom it succeeds in influencing and dominating. One characteristic is this: it covets praise. It feeds and fattens on commendation. It constantly seeks to be highly esteemed, to have its worth properly appraised. It is immensely impressed with its own importance, its value to society, its keenness, wisdom or aptness, and wishes others to be so impressed also. It is fond of a mirror, especially one made to magnify. It seeks recognition. It presses forward, rudely or politely, according as its habitat has been trained in rude or polite circles. It may put on the garb of humility, and use the language of depreciation. But its ear is none the less keenly alert to hear the agreeable things and to cherish them.

Another characteristic, which really is simply the other side of this first-named one, is this: it shrinks from criticism. How it writhes and twists at the least touch of unfavourable criticism! It is always on the defensive. The cheek colours at the suggestion of its being wrong, or having blundered, or of being peculiar.

How quickly it explains and defends and brings evidence of its being in the right. It is extremely sensitive. It is that touchy thing in you. It is chronically troubled with the disease of touchiness. It has an interrogation point constantly on sentinel duty, namely, 'What will they think?' 'What will they say?' It lives in constant fear, under the lash of that huge, vague, awful 'they.' Its feelings are readily hurt. It is easily slighted. It remembers grievances.

I remember knowing a Sunday School teacher who had a mission class of rather rough boys from non-Christian homes. I asked one day how she was getting along with them. 'Going to give them up,' she replied. 'Is that so? They have all become Christians?' No, none of them were Christians, and they liked her, and said they would not come if she gave them up, but she felt discouraged, and anyway she had decided to give them up. Lawyers and women do not always give their reasons. I ventured to suggest that before giving them up she should have the boys come up to her home, one at a time, perhaps for tea; have a pleasant chatty time at tea and afterwards, and then before the boy left have a quiet, friendly talk with him by himself about being a Christian, and a few words of prayer with him. Wouldn't she try that before giving them up? And I remember distinctly that her face blushed as red as a bright red rose as she replied, 'Why, Mr. Gordon, he'd laugh at me!' And she could not bear the possible chance of being laughed at for the other more likely possibility of winning a soul—a man—a life. That was 'self' in her, shrinking back from a laugh; dreading that look of possibly contemptuous surprise that might come.

Another person, speaking about certain recreations very common in society, and which he was in the habit of joining, though freely questioning the propriety of so doing, said, 'Oh, I don't care much for those things. I could easily give them up, but people think you are so queer if you decline, and you feel as if you were a back number.' Ah! there was the rub. The desire to be thought well of; the dislike of being considered peculiar; the fear of that thinly veiled sneering curl on the lip— that was 'self' in him asserting its presence, and even more, ruling his action. Do you recognize the individual inside of you that Jesus is speaking of?

There is a third tell-tale ear-mark of self that is difficult to conceal—it is assertive. It dearly loves to have its own way. It has plans and ambitions, and proposes to carry them through regardless of man, or—let the plain truth be spoken softly—of God. Its opinions are held tenaciously. Its favourite pronoun is 'I,' capitalised, with variations of 'my' and 'me'. The personal equation is extremely powerful and persuasive.

The true follower of Jesus holds every plan 'subject to

10

change' from above. But this self, if allowed to rule, takes the bit in its tightly-shut teeth, and drives determinedly ahead, reckless of either man's or God's preferences, even though religious phraseology may be upon its tongue.

Still another trait of character of this self whose closer acquaintance we are making is this: it has an insatiable appetite. It grows hungrier by that on which it feeds. Its capacity is beyond the measuring line. If given free rein it will debase the holiest functions of the body, and degrade the highest powers of the mind to appease its gnawing, passion-bitten hunger. The noblest gifts, the purest emotions, the most sacred relationships, are dragged down to the slimy gutter to tempt and temporarily stay its jaded palate.

That is something of a suggestion of the character of this other master than Jesus, who seeks to get control of us, and from whose relentless, vice-like grip Jesus would fain free us. He says there is only one thing to do with it. No half-way compromise—the great American expedient —will do here. The Master says plainly it is to be denied, repressed, put determinedly down, starved, strangled. To every suggestion or demand there is to be a prompt, positive, jaw-locked 'no'.

There is war to the knife, and the knife clear up to the hilt, between these two claimants for the control of our powers—self and Jesus. Paul understood this antagonism thoroughly. It comes out repeatedly in his writings. His name for this inner enemy, by an accidental turn in English, is Jesus' word 'self' spelled backwards with the letter 'h' added—f-l-e-s-h. His remarks in Romans, eighth chapter, verses four to eight, and twelve to thirteen, are simply an enlargement of these words in the sixteenth of Matthew's Gospel. If one will read these verses, substituting Jesus' word self for Paul's word he will be surprised to find how strikingly Paul is expressing this very thought of Jesus. A free translation of part of these verses would read like this: Verse five—'They that choose to walk after self (as a slave walked after, or behind, his master) will show their choice by obeying the desires of self, and they that choose to walk after the Spirit will obey the desires of the Spirit.' Verse seven—'For the purposes of self are opposed to God's purposes; for it does not hold itself subject to God's wishes; indeed, in its very nature it cannot; and they that choose to obey self cannot please God.' Verse thirteen—'If by the Holy Spirit's aid ye kill off the plans and doings of self, ye shall therein find real true life, and only so.'

Plainly, the deep searching experiences of Paul's great soul, and his wide observation of others, in his ceaseless travels, confirm the statements already made, that there is the intense hatred, the bitterest antagonism, between these two personalities represented by Jesus' words 'himself' and 'Me'. There can be no patched-up truce here. The only way the lion and the lamb can lie down together in this case is for the one to lie down underneath the other—conquered; or inside the other—devoured.

In his other letters, Paul sometimes uses still another name, 'the old man', and names the characteristics of this omnipresent self, which crop out with varying degrees of prominence, in different persons, and under different circumstances. Notice only a few of these: In Galatians, fifth chapter, nineteenth verse: 'The deeds of self are . . . improper sexual intercourse, impurity, shameless loose-ness. . . .' It will, wherever possible, debase the holiest functions of the body. In Colossians, third chapter, fifth verse, speaking of the old man: 'And covetousness, which is reckoning of highest worth that which is less worthy than God.' That is to say, the ambitious longings of self, will if unchecked become the ruling passion, thrusting all else ruthlessly aside and degrading the highest powers of the mind to satisfying its feverish desire. In Ephesians, fourth chapter, thirty-first verse: 'Bitterness, passion, anger, loud disputing, evil-speaking . . . malice.' Its assertiveness, and demand for a due recognition of its worth, its rights, its opinions, its proper place, bring bitterest burnings, and worse. It will not be needful to review recent world events, or common congressional, and political, and society life for illustrations. They may be found much nearer one's own door.

Was there ever such a list? Such a being whose heart begets and nurses such progeny! This being has the smell of hell, and of the evil one himself. Ah! now we are getting at the straight truth. Self is Satan's personal representative in every human heart. It gets in through the only door by which it ever can gain an entrance, namely, the door of disobedience. How keen Jesus was in recognizing the suggester of the thought that found expression through Peter's lips—'Get thee behind me, Satan.' Self is Satan, condensed into each man's life, though in some he dare not exhibit his coarser traits; and in others he is being constantly conquered by that power of the spirit of Jesus which comes through absolute, glad surrender to Him.

This sly Satan-self may often be recognized by a favourite question it asks among Christian people about a great many so-called unimportant matters:—'What's the harm?' But a true follower of Jesus never lives down upon the plane of what's-the-harm? He lives up in a higher sphere with his Master, who pleased not Himself, but made it the steady, unfaltering aim of His life to do always those things that were pleasing to His Father.

Men thought Him narrow and fanatical, but He cared not so long as He could daily hear that clear, sweet voice saying 'this is My beloved Son, in Whom I am well pleased.' The final touchstone which the follower of Jesus applies to every matter is this: Would it please Him?

Let everyone here who earnestly desires to fit into, and to fill out, Jesus' plan for his life, take paper and pencil and make a list of his personal habits; such as his eating, what he eats and how; his drinking, other things he puts into his mouth, his dress, the use and care of his body, his recreations, his reading, his conversation, his use of money, his use of time, his life plans and his daily plans, his social engagements; and regarding each ask plainly the question—what is the motive that controls me in this? Is it my own preference or enjoyment? or, is it to please and honour Jesus? Let him further go through the list of his business methods, his friendships, the various organizations he belongs to, with the same question. If he will do thorough work he will probably have some stiff fighting on hand both at the start and afterwards. Many a life would thereby be radically changed. For example, I know a Christian storekeeper who has on his shelves a certain article bearing the label of a tonic medicine. But he knows perfectly well, as does anyone who stops to think about it, that the stuff back of the label is one form of an intoxicant. There can be no question of what the Master would say about it. But it brings a good profit. And his money-fevered self asserts its mastery and carries the day. And the man tightly grips the profits, while Satan chuckles with unholy glee, and souls are being damned by this Christian man's aid. Certainly there can be none of the power of God in such a life. Let us rather speak the truth and say that this man is exerting a positive power for Satan and hell.

All this is included in these few simple words, let him deny himself. Is there still a fixed purpose to follow Jesus without regard to what it may cost us, or where the keen edge of separation may cut in?

Here is a forking of the road. I bring all my readers up to this dividing, and therefore deciding, point. Let each choose his own road deliberately, prayerfully, with open eyes. This road to the left has as its law, yielding to self; saying yes to the desires and demands of self; with some modifications possibly, here and there, for I am talking to professing Christian people: 'Yes' to Jesus sometimes, but at other times, when it suits circumstances and inclinations better to do otherwise—well, a pushing of the troublesome question aside. And that means a decided yes to self, with as positive a negative to Jesus' desires implied thereby. That is the left-hand fork.

This right-hand road knows only one law to which exception is never made, namely: *Yes to Jesus*, everywhere, always, regardless of consequences, though it may entail loss of friendships, or money, or position, or social standing, or personal preferences, or radical change of plans, or what not.

Judas assented to the cravings of his ambitious self and said no to his Master, thinking possibly, with his worldly shrewdness, thereby to force Jesus to assert His power. He little knew what a time of crisis it was, and what terrific results would follow.

Peter stood on the side of his cowardly, shrinking self in the courtyard that dark night, and against his Master. And though with matchless love he was forgiven, he never forgave himself, nor was able to get that night's doings out of his memory. Judas and Peter were brothers in action that night, and there are evidences that many other disciples are standing over in the same group. Are you? Which road do you choose: this—to the left? Or, this—to the right?

I knew a young man who was deeply attached to an admirable young woman, both refined Christian persons, much above the average in native ability, and in culture. He made known to her his feelings. But as strong women are apt to do, she held him off, testing him repeatedly, to find out just how real his attachment was. Finally revealing indirectly her own feeling she still withheld the consent he pleaded for, until he would yield acquiescence in a certain plan of hers for him. The plan proper enough in itself, was an ambitious one, and tended decidedly toward swinging him away from the high, tenderly spiritual ideals that had swayed his life in college and afterwards, though he probably was not clearly conscious of this tendency. The only safe thing to do under such strong circumstances was to take time, aside, alone, for calm, poised, thought and prayer, to learn if her plan was also the Master's plan for him. But the personal element proved too strong for such deliberation. The possibility of losing her swung him off his feet. It was no longer a question between her plan and the Master's plan. The latter dropped out of view, probably half unconsciously because hurriedly. *He* must have her, he thought. That rose before his eyes above all else. And so the decision was made. With what result? He is to-day prominent in Christian service, an earnest speaker, a tireless worker, with a most winsome personality. But his inner spiritual life has perceptibly dwarfed. His ideals, still high and noble, are distinctly lower than in his earlier life. Intellectual ideals, admirable in themselves, but belonging to second place in a Christian life, now command the field. His conceptions and understanding of spiritual truth have undergone a decided change.

The proposal of the self-life came in very fascinating guise to him. He hastily said yes to it: that meant as decided a refusal of Another's plan for him, which had once been clearly recognized, and accepted, but was now set aside, be it sadly said, as he swung quickly off to the left fork of the road.

There is an incident told of a European pastor, an earnest, eloquent man. The realization came in upon him that he had not been fully following the Master. In much of his life self was still ruling. He came to this forking of the road, and the battle was a fierce one, for self dies hard. But finally 'by the Spirit,' he got the victory, as everyone may, and calmly stepped off to the right. He has vividly described that battle of the forks in language, the accuracy of which will be recognized by others who have been in action on that field.

> Oh, the bitter shame and sorrow,
>   That a time could ever be
> When I let the Saviour's pity
> Plead in vain, and proudly answered:
>   "*All of self, and none of Thee.*"
>
> Yet He found me: I beheld Him
>   Bleeding on the accursed tree;
> Heard Him pray, "Forgive them, Father,"
> And my wistful heart said faintly:
>   "*Some of self and some of Thee.*"
>
> Day by day His tender mercy,
>   Healing, helping, full and free,
> Sweet and strong, and oh, so patient,
> Brought me lower, while I whispered:
>   "*Less of self and more of Thee.*"

> Higher than the highest heaven,
>   Deeper than the deepest sea,
> Lord, *Thy love* at last has conquered;
> Grant me now my soul's desire,
>   *"None of self and all of Thee."*

Is there still a fixed purpose? Will you take this right fork? Let those who linger reluctantly and those who will listen to the further word that Jesus adds: 'Let him deny himself and take up his cross.' *Take up his cross*—what does that mean? The cross has come to be regarded in those days as a fine ornament. It looks beautiful bejewelled; on the end of a sword; or worked into regalia. It makes such an artistic finish to a church building, finely chiselled in stone, or enwreathed with ivy. It looks pretty in jewellery and flowers. But to Jesus and the men of His time it had a grim, hard, painful significance. In Roman usage a man condemned to death was required to take up the crude wooden cross provided, carry it out to the place of execution, and there be transfixed upon it. Plainly to these men listening, Jesus' words meant: Let him say 'no' to his self, and then nail it up on the cross and leave it there *to die*.

Paul understood this thoroughly. To help the young Christians in Galatia he explains his own experience by saying: 'I have been crucified with Christ'; and to the unknown friends in Rome he writes: 'If ye by the Spirit put to death the doings of the self life ye shall live.' The only thing to do with this self is to kill it.

In Luke's account an intensely practical word is added to Jesus' remark: 'Let him take up his cross daily.' A cat is said to have nine lives, because it is so hard to kill. I do not know what your experience may have been, but, judged by this rule, the self in me is tougher-lived than that. It has about ninety-nine, or nine hundred and ninety-nine lives. I put it on the cross to-day in the purpose of my will by the power of the Spirit, and I find it trying to sneak down and step into active control again to-morrow through some sly, subtle suggestion which it hopes may get past the vigilance of my sentinel. That word daily becomes, of necessity, my constant keynote— a daily conflict, a daily sleepless vigilance, and, thank God, a daily victory.

Every man's heart is a battlefield. If self has possession, Jesus is lovingly striving to get possession. If possession has been yielded to Jesus, there is a constant besieging by the forces of self. And self is a skilled strategist. In every heart there is a cross, and a throne, and each is occupied. If Jesus is on the throne, ruling, self is on the cross, dying. But if self is being obeyed, and so is ruling, then it is on the throne. And self on the throne means that Jesus has been put on the Cross. And it seems to be only too pathetically true that not only in New Testament times, but in these times, there are numbers of professing Christians, who, in the practice of daily life, are crucifying the Son of God afresh, and openly exposing Him to shame before the eyes of the crowd.

Suppose that now I determine to make this absolute surrender to Jesus, as my Master. To-morrow in some matter, possibly a small matter—speaking a word to someone—asking a silent blessing at the meal—making a change in some personal habit—or some other apparently trivial matter—the Spirit quietly makes clear His wish as to what I should do. But I hesitate: it seems hard. I do not say that I will not obey, but actually I do not. Let me plainly understand that in such a single failure to obey, self is again mounting the throne, and through the experiences of the wilderness temptation, and of Gethsemane, and of Calvary, but it will also be to share the victory which was always coupled with every testing *He* met. It will as certainly be following Him in power, and victory, on past Calvary to the new life of the resurrection morning, that saw the greatest display of power. And even past that, to the upper chamber where His words burn their way into our hearts—'as the Father sent Me (clothed with power unconquerable) even so send I you.' And then to Olivet, where the victorious words ring out, 'All power hath been given unto Me in heaven and on earth, therefore go ye and make disciples.'

> If any man
> would come after Me,
> let him say 'no' to his self,
> and nail it to the cross daily,
> and follow Me.

Jesus, Master, by the Holy Spirit's help, *I will*.

POWER

WHAT ARE ITS EFFECTS?

A FLOOD-TIDE is a rising tide. It flows in and fills up and spreads out. Wherever it goes it cleanses and fertilises and beautifies. For untold centuries Egypt has depended for its very life upon the yearly flood-tide of the Nile. The rich bottom lands of the Connecticut valley are refertilised every spring by that river's flood-tide. The green beauty and rich fruitage of some parts of the Sacramento Valley, whose soil is flooded by the artificial irrigation-rivers, are in sharp contrast with adjoining unwatered portions.

The flood-tide is caused by influences from above. In the ocean and the portions of rivers under its influence by the heavenly bodies. In the rivers by the fall of rain and snow swelling successively the upper streams and lakes.

God's highest ideal for men is frequently expressed under the figure of a river running at flood-tide. Ezekiel's vision of the future capital of Israel gives prominence to a wonderful river gradually reaching flood-tide and exerting untold influence.

John's companion vision of the future church in the closing chapters of Revelation finds its radiating centre in an equally wonderful river of water of life. When Jesus would give a picture of a Christian man up to His ideal He exclaims, 'Out of his belly shall flow rivers of living water.' John's explanation years after was that He was speaking of the Holy Spirit's presence in the human life. Jesus' ideal would put our lives at the flood-tide. No ebb-tide there. No rise and fall. But a constant flowing in and filling up and flooding out.

It has been said that the companion word to surrender is mastery. My surrender to Jesus carries with it His mastery over me. We may have tried to get some closer knowledge of Him who assumes mastery. Now, we need to get some clear idea of the results of His unrestrained presence. It is not surprising that there have been some mistaken ideas about the results. It has been a common supposition that somehow the baptism of the Holy Spirit is always connected with an evangelistic gift, and with marked success in soul-winning. Men have thought of Mr. Moody facing great crowds, who were swayed and melted at his words, and of people in great multitudes accepting Christ. Probably the world has never had a finer illustration of a Spirit-filled man than in dear old Moody. And it is not to be wondered at that the rare evangelistic gift of service with which he was endowed and the great results attending it should be so closely allied in our minds with the Spirit-filled life which he exemplified so unusually. In sharp contrast with such a conception, however, are the results in some of the Spirit-swayed men whom God used in Bible times. Isaiah was called to a service that was to be barren of results, and Jeremiah's was not only fruitless but with great personal peril. Jesus' public work led through a rough path to a crown of thorns and a cross. Stephen's testimony brought him a storm of stones. And Paul passed through great danger and distress to a cell, and beyond to a keen-edged axe. These are leaders among Spirit-filled men.

Paul's teaching in the Corinthian epistle helps one to a clear understanding about results. He explains that while it is one Spirit dwelling in all who acknowledge

Jesus as Lord, yet the evidence of His presence differs widely in different persons. It is one God working all things in all persons, but with great variety in the gifts bestowed, in the service with which they are entrusted, and in the inner experiences they are conscious of.

What results then may be expected to follow the filling of the Holy Spirit? It may be said in a sentence that Jesus fills us with the same Spirit that filled Himself that He may work out in us His own image and ideal, and make use of us in His passionate reaching out after others. If we attempt to analyse these results we shall find them falling into three groups. First—results in the life, that is in the inner experiences, and the habits. Second—results in the personality that is in the appearance, and the mental faculties. Third—results in service. Let us look a little at each of these.

Without doubt the first result experienced will be a new sense of peace: a glad, quiet stillness of spirit which nothing seems able to disturb. The heart will be filled with a peace still as the stars, calm as the night, deep as the sea, fragrant as the flowers.

How many thousands of lips have lovingly lingered over those sweet strong words: 'the peace of God, which passeth all understanding, shall guard your heart and thought in Christ Jesus.' It is God's peace. It acts as an armed guard drawn up around heart and thoughts to keep unrest out. It is too subtle for intellectual analysis, but it steals into and steadies the heart. You cannot understand it but you can feel it. You cannot get hold of it with your head, but you can with your heart. You do not get it. It gets you. You need not understand in order to experience. Blessed are they that have not understood and yet have yielded and experienced.

Spirit given unto us' (Rom. 5. 5). The all inclusive result is love. That marvellous tender passion—the love of God—heightless, depthless, shoreless, shall flood our hearts, making us as gentle and tenderhearted, and self-sacrificing and gracious as He. Every phase of life will become a phase of love. Peace is love resting. Bible study is love reading its lover's letters. Prayer is love keeping tryst. Conflict with sin is love jealously fighting for its lover. Hatred of sin is love shrinking from that which separates from its lover. Sympathy is love tenderly feeling. Enthusiasm is love burning. Hope is love expecting. Patience is love waiting. Faithfulness is love sticking fast. Humility is love taking its true place. Modesty is love keeping out of sight. Soul-winning is love pleading.

Love is revolutionary. It radically changes us, and revolutionises our spirit toward all others. Love is democratic. It ruthlessly levels all class distinctions. Love is intensely practical. It is always hunting something to do. Paul lays great stress on this outer practical side. Do you remember his 'fruit of the Spirit?' It is an analysis of love. While the first three—love, joy, peace—are emotions within, the remaining six are outward toward others. Notice, long suffering, gentleness, goodness, faithfulness, meekness, and then the climax is reached in the last—self-control. And in the great love passage in the first Corinthian epistle, he picks out four of these last six and shows further just what he means by love in its practical working in the life. Long-suffering is repeated, and so is kindness or goodness. Faithfulness is reproduced in 'never faileth.' Then self-control receives the emphasis of an eight-fold repetition of 'nots'. Listen—Envieth not, boasteth not, not puffed up, not unseemly, seeketh not (even) her own, is not provoked, taketh not account of evil (in trying to help others, like Jesus' word 'despairing of no man'), rejoiceth not in unrighteousness (that is when the unrighteous is punished, but instead feels sorry for him). What tremendous power of self-mastery in those 'nots!' Then the positive side is brought out in four 'alls'; two of them —the first and last—passive qualities, 'beareth all things,' 'endureth all things.' And in between, two active 'hopeth all things', 'believeth all things'. The passive qualities doing sentinel duty on both sides of the active. These passive traits are intensely active in their passivity. There is a busy time under the surface of those nots and alls. What a wealth of underlying power they reveal! Sometimes folks think it sentimental to talk of love. Probably it is of some stuff that shuffles along under that name. But when the Holy Spirit talks about it, and fills our hearts with it there is seen to be an intensely practical passion at work.

Love is not only the finest fruit but it is the final test of a Christian life. How many splendid men of God have seemed to lack here. What a giant of faith and strength Elijah was. Such intense indignation over sin! Such fearless denunciation! What tremendous faith gripping the very heavens! What marvellous power in prayer! Yet listen to him criticising the faithful remnant whom God lovingly defends against his aspersions. There seems a serious lack there. God seems to understand his need. He asks him to slip down to Horeb for a new vision of his Master. And then He revealed Himself not in whirlwind nor earthquake nor lightning. He doubtless felt at home among these tempestuous outbreaks. They suit his temper. But something startlingly new came to him in that exquisite 'sound of gentle stillness,' hushing, aweing, mellowing, giving a new conception of the dominant heart of his God. Some of us might well drop things, and take a run down to Horeb.

I know an earnest scholarly minister with strong personality, and fearless in his preaching against sin, but who seems to lack this spirit of love. He is so cuttingly critical at times. The other ministers of his town whom he might easily lead, shy off from him. There is no magnetism in the edge of a razor. His critical spirit can be felt when his lips are shut. I recall a woman, earnest, winsome when she chooses, an intelligent Bible student, keen-scented for error, a generous giver, but what a sharp edge her tongue has. One is afraid to get close lest it may cut.

When the Holy Ghost takes possession there is *love*, aye, more, a *flood* of it. Have you ever seen a flood? I remember one in the Schuykill during my boyhood days and how it impressed me. Those who live along the valley of that treacherous mountain stream, the Ohio, know something of the power of a flood. How the waters come rushing down, cutting out new channels, washing down rubbish, tearing valuable property from its moorings, ruling the valley autocratically while men stand back perfectly helpless.

Would you care to have a flood-tide of love flush the channelways of your life like that? It would clean out something you have preferred keeping. It would with quiet, ruthless strength, tear some prized possessions from their moorings and send them adrift down stream and out. Its high waters would put out some of the fires on the lower levels. Better think a bit before opening the sluice-ways for that flood. But, ah! it will sweeten and make fragrant. It will cut new channels, and broaden and deepen old ones. And what a harvest will follow in its wake. Floods are apt to do peculiar things. So does this one. It washes out the friction-grit from between the wheels. It does not dull the edge of the tongue, but washes the bitter out of the mouth, and the green out of the eye. It leaves one deaf and blind in some matters, but much keener-sighted and quicker eared in others. Strange flood that! Would that we all knew more of it.

Now note some of the changes in the personality which attend the Spirit's unrestrained presence. Without doubt the face will change, though it might be difficult to describe the change. That Spirit within changes the look of the eye. His peace within the heart will affect the flow of blood in the physical heart, and so in turn the clearness of the complexion. The real secret of winsome beauty is here. That new dominant purpose will modulate the voice, and the whole expression of the face, and the touch of the hand, and the carriage of the body. And yet the one changed will be least conscious of it, if conscious at all. Neither Moses nor Stephen knew of their transfigured faces.

It is of peculiar interest to note the changes in the mental make-up. It may be said positively that the original group of mental faculties remain the same. There seems to be nothing to indicate that any change takes place in one's natural endowment. No faculty is added that nature had not put there, and certainly none removed.

But it is very clear that there is a marked development of these natural gifts, and that this change is brought about by the putting in of a new and tremendous motive power, which radically affects everything it touches.

Regarding this development four facts may be noted.

First fact: Those faculties or talents which may hitherto have lain latent, unmatured, are aroused into use. Most men have large undeveloped resources, and endowments. Many of us are one-sided in our development. We are strangers to the real possible self within, unconscious of some of the powers with which we are endowed and entrusted. The Holy Spirit, when given a free hand, works out the fulness of the life that has been put in. The change will not be in the sort but in the size, and that not by an addition but by a growth of what is there.

Moses complains that he is slow of speech and of a slow tongue. God does not promise a new tongue but that he will be *with* Him and *train* his tongue. Listen to him forty years after in the Moab Plain, as with brain fired, and tongue loosened and trained he gives that series of farewell talks fairly burning with eloquence. Students of oratory can find no nobler specimens than Deuteronomy furnishes. The unmatured powers lying dormant had been aroused to full growth by the indwelling Spirit of God.

Saintly Dr. A. J. Gordon, whose face was as surely transfigured as was Moses' or Stephen's, used to say that in his earlier years he had no executive ability. Men would say of him, 'Well, Gordon can preach but——' intimating that he could not do much else; not much of the practical getting of things done in his make-up. When he was offered the chairmanship of the missionary committee of the Baptist Church, he promptly declined as being utterly unfit for such a task. Finally with reluctance he accepted, and for years he guided and moulded with rare sagacity the entire scheme of missionary operation of the great Baptist Church of the North. He was accustomed with rare frankness and modesty to speak of the change in himself as an illustration of how the Spirit develops talents which otherwise had lain unsuspected and unused.

Second fact: *ALL* faculties will be developed to the

highest normal pitch. Not only the undeveloped faculties, but those already developed will know a new life.
That new presence within will sharpen the brain, and
fire the imagination. It will make the logic keener, the
will steadier, the executive faculty more alert.

The civil engineer will be more accurate in his measure-
ments and calculations. The scientific man more keenly
observant of facts, better poised in his generalisation
upon them, and more convincing in his demonstrations.
The locomotive engineer will handle his huge machine
more skilfully. The road saves money in having a
Christian hand on the throttle. The lawyer will be more
thorough in his sifting of evidence, and more convincing
in the planning of his cases. The business man will be
even more sharply alive to business. The college student
can better grasp his studies, and write with stronger
thought and clearer diction. The cook will get a finer
flavour into the food. And so on to the end of the list.
Why? Not by any magic, but simply and only because
man was created to be animated and dominated by the
Spirit of God. That is his normal condition. The Spirit
of God is his natural atmosphere. The machine works
best when run under the inventor's immediate direction.
Only as a man—any man—is swayed by the Holy Spirit,
will his powers rise to their best. And a man is not doing
his best, however hardworking and conscientious, and
therefore not fair to his own powers, who lives otherwise.

Third fact: There will be a gradual bringing back to
their normal condition of those faculties which have been
dwarfed or warped, or abnormally developed through
sin and selfishness. Sometimes these moral twists and
quirks in our mental faculties are an inheritance through
one or more generations. The man with excessive
egotism often carries the evidence of it in the very shape

of his head. But as he yields to the new Spirit dominant within, a spirit of humility, of modesty, will gradually displace so much of the other as is abnormal. The man of superficial mind will be deepened in his mental processes. The man of hasty judgment or poor judgment will grow careful in his conclusions. The lazy man will get a new lease of ambition and energy.

These results will be gradual, as all of God's processes are. Sometimes painfully gradual, and will be strictly in proportion as the man yields himself unreservedly to the control of the indwelling Spirit. And the process of doing it will be by the injection of a new and mighty motive power. The shallow-minded man will have an intense desire to study God's wondrous classic so as to learn His will. And though his studies may not get much farther, yet no one Book so disciplines and deepens the mind as that. The lazy man will find a fire kindling in his bones to please his Master and do something for Him, and that will burn through and burn up his indolence. The man of hasty judgment will find himself stopping to consider what his Master would desire. And the mere pause to think is a long step toward more accurate judgment. He will become a reverent student of the Word of God, and nothing corrects the judgment like that.

The self-willed, headstrong man will likely have the toughest time of any. To let his own plan utterly go, and instead fit into a radically different one will shake him up terrifically. But that mighty One within will lovingly woo and move him. And as he yields, and victory comes, he will be delighted to find that the highest act of the strongest will is to yield to a higher will when found. He will be charmed to discover that the rarest liberty comes only in perfect obedience to perfect law.

And so every sort of man who has got some moral twist or obliquity in his mental make-up will be straightened out to the normal standard of his Maker, as he allows Him to take full control.

The fourth fact: All this growth and development will be strictly along the groove of the man's natural endowment. The natural mental bent will not be changed though the moral crooks will be straightened out. Peter's rash, self-assertive twists are corrected, but he remains the same Peter mentally. He does not possess the rare logical powers of Paul, nor the judicial administrative temper of James before the infilling, and is not endowed with either after that experience. John's intensity which would call down fire to burn up supposed foes is not removed but turned into another channel, and burns itself out in love. Jonathan Edwards retains and develops his marvellous faculty of metaphysical reasoning and uses it to influence men for God. Finney's intensely logical mind is not changed but fired and used in the same direction.

Moody has neither of these gifts, but has an unusually magnetic presence, and a great executive faculty which leaves its impress on his blunt direct speech. His faculties are not changed, nor added to, but developed wonderfully and used. George Muller never becomes a great preacher like these three, nor an expositor, but finds his rare development in his marked administrative skill. Charles Studd remains a poor speaker with jagged rhetoric and with no organising knack, though the fire of God in his very presence kindles the flames of mission zeal in the British universities, and melts your very heart as you listen. Shaftesbury's mental processes show the generations of aristocratic breeding even in his costermonger's cart lovingly winning these men, or after midnight searching out the waifs of London's nooks and docks. Clough is refused by the missionary board because of his lack of certain required qualifications, and when finally he reaches the field none of these qualities appear, but his skill as an engineer gives him a hold upon thousands whom his presence and God-breathed passion for souls win to Jesus Christ. Carey's unusual linguistic talent, William Thaw's genius for business, Mary Lyon's teaching gift are not changed, but developed and used. The growth produced by the Spirit's presence is strictly along the groove of the natural gift. But note that in this great variety of natural endowment there is one trait— a moral trait, not a mental—that marks all alike, namely a pervading purpose that comes to be a passion to do God's will, and get men to know Him, and that everything is forced to bend to this dominant purpose. *Is not this glorious unity in diversity?*

The third group of results affects our service. We will want to serve. Love must act. We must do something for our Master. We must do something for those around us. There will be a new spirit of service. Its peculiar characteristic and charm will be the heart of love in it. Love will envelop and undergird and pervade and exude from all service. There will be a fine graciousness, a patience, a strong tenderness, an earnest faithfulness, a hopeful tirelessness which will despair of no man, and no situation.

The sort of service and the sphere of service will be left entirely to the direction of the indwelling Holy Spirit, 'dividing to every man *as He will*.' There will be no choosing of a life work but a prayerful waiting till *His choice* is clear, and then a joyous acceptance of that. There will be no attempt to open doors, not even with a single touch or twist of the knob, but only an entering of *opened* doors.

If the work be humble, or the place lowly, or both, there will be a cheery eager using of the highest powers keyed to their best pitch. If higher up, a steady remembering that there can be no power save as the Spirit controls, and a praying to be kept from the dizziness which unaccustomed height is apt to produce. Large quantities of paper and ink will be saved. For many letters of application and endorsement will remain unwritten.

The Master's say-so is accepted by Spirit-led men as final. He chooses Peter to *open* the door to the outer nations, and Paul to *enter* the opened door. He chooses not an apostle but Philip to open up Samaria, and Titus to guide church matters in Crete. A miner's son is chosen to shake Europe, and a cobbler to kindle anew the missionary fires of Christendom. Livingstone is sent to open up the heart of Africa for a fresh infusion of the blood of the Son of God. A nursemaid, whose name remains unknown, is used to mould for God the child who became the seventh Earl of Shaftesbury, one of the most truly Spirit-filled men of the world. George Muller is chosen for the signal service of re-teaching men that God still lives and actually answers prayer. Speer is used to breathe a new spirit of devotion among college students, and Mott to arouse and organise their service around the world. George Williams and Robert M'Burney becomes the leaders, British and American, in an in-Spirited movement to win young men by thousands. An earnest woman is chosen to mother and to shape for God the tender years of earth's greatest Queen, who through character and position exerted a greater influence for righteousness than any other woman. The common factor in all is the Chooser. Jesus is the Chief Executive of the Campaign through His Spirit. The direction of it belongs to Him. He knows best what each one can do. He knows best what needs to be done. He is ambitious that each of us shall be the best, and have the best. He has a plan thought out for each life, and for the whole campaign. His Spirit is in us to administer His plan. He never sleeps. He divideth to every man severally as He will. And His is a loving, wise will. It can be trusted.

A Spirit-mastered man slowly comes to understand that service now is apprenticeship-service. He is in training for the time when a King shall reign, and will need tested and trusted and trained servants. He is in college getting ready for commencement day. That may explain in part why some of the workers whom we think can be least spared, are called away in their prime. Their apprentice term is served. School's out. They are moved up.

Please remember that these are flood-tide results. Some good people will never know them except in a very limited way. For they do not open the sluice gates wide enough to let the waters reach flood-tide. These results will vary in degree with the degree and constancy of the yielding to the Spirit's control. A full yielding at the start, and constantly continued will bring these results in full measure and without break, though the growth will be gradual. For it is a rising flood, ever increasing in height and depth and sweep and power. Partial surrender will mean only partial results; the largest and finest results come only as the Spirit has full control, for the work is all His, by and with our consent.

In one of her exquisite poems Frances Ridley Havergal tells of a friend who was given an Æolian harp which, she was told, sent out unutterably sweet melodies. She tried to bring the music by playing upon it with her hand, but found the seven strings would yield but one tone. Keenly disappointed she turned to the letter sent before the gift and found she had not noticed the directions given. Following them carefully she placed the harp in the opened window-way where the wind could blow upon it. Quite a while she waited but at last in the twilight the music came:

> Like stars that tremble into light
> Out of the purple dark, a low, sweet note
> Just trembled out of silence, antidote
>   To any doubt; for never finger might
> Produce that note, so different, so new;
> Melodious pledge that all He promised should
>   come true.

> Anon a thrill of all the strings:
> And then a flash of music, swift and bright,
> Like a first throb of wierd Auroral light,
>   Then crimson coruscation from the wings
> Of the Pole-spirit; then ecstatic beat,
> As if an angel-host went forth on shining feet.

> Soon passed the sounding starlit march,
> And then one swelling note grew full and long,
> While, like a far-off cathedral song,
>   Through dreamy length of echoing aisle and arch
> Float softest harmonies around, above,
> Like flowing chordal robes of blessing and of love.

> Thus, while the holy stars did shine
> And listen, the Æolian marvels breathed,
> While love and peace and gratitude enwreathed
>   With rich delight in one fair crown were mine.
> The wind that bloweth where it listeth brought
> This glory of harp-music—not my skill or thought.

And the listening friend to whom this wondrous experience is told, who has had a great sorrow in her life, and been much troubled in her thoughts and plans, replies:

> . . . I, too, have tried
> My finger skill in vain. But opening now
> My window, like wise Daniel, I will set
> My little harp therein, and listening wait
> The breath of heaven, the Spirit of our God.

Can we, too, learn the lesson of the wind-harp? *For man is God's Æolian harp.* The human-taught finger skill can bring some rare music, yet by comparison 'tis at best but a monotone. When the instrument is set to catch the full breathing of the breath of God, then shall it sound out the rarest wealth of music's melodies.

How amazing it is that Jesus crucified, risen, glorified can do much more by far in us by the Holy Spirit than He could in person on earth in the days of His flesh. It is as though the Lord Jesus had actually come back again and we had Him all to ourselves—and more.

But how can we know this experience of the Holy Spirit, the love-gift of the Lord Jesus Christ? Surrender to Him to be changed and cleansed and used as He may choose. Then, filled with His presence we can sing:

> I have a wonderful guest,
> Who speeds my feet, who moves my hands,
> Who strengthens, comforts, guides, commands,
> Whose presence gives me rest.

Thus as the life is yielded fully to the breathing of the Spirit we shall find the peace of God which passeth all understanding, filling the heart; and the power of God that passeth all resisting flooding the life; and others shall find the beauty of God, that passeth all describing, transfiguring the face; and the dewy fragrance of God, that passeth all comparing, pervading the personality, though most likely *we* shall not know it.

SERVICE

My hands were strong in fancied strength,
  But not in power divine,
And bold to take up tasks at length,
  That were not His but mine.
The Master came and touched my hands
  (And might was in His own!)
But mine since then have powerless been,
  Save His are laid thereon,
    'And it is only thus,' said He,
  'That I can work My works through thee.'

SERVICE

WHAT ARE THE TOOLS?

THE beginning of all service is the personal touch with our Lord Jesus Christ as Saviour, and Lord, and Friend. Then there must needs be an equipment for service, as a second thing. There are three things that are absolutely essential to our equipment for service. There may be a personal touch with Him as Saviour and Master, and yet very limited power in service, or almost no power. There *may* be many other things beside these three things. There *must* be these three.

Some of you, doubtless, are glad to give great gifts with which you may have been endowed, to our Master's service. Some are glad to serve in humbler service. Some have trained brains, and special advantages by nature and by education; there must be all of that, for much service that has to be done. But whether your sphere is more prominent, or very humble, there must be these three things. I shall name them in order, ascending from the least, though the least is not small but large.

The first thing is this, *there must be a grip upon this blessed Word of God*. And if you ask what I mean by that word 'grip', I say this—the meaning runs on a sliding scale, because the closer grip you get the more you feel how much there is you have not gotten. Your grip may be very small, yet through it the Master uses you. And no matter how great the grip may become, in keenness and tenacity, in intelligence, and all of that, there must needs be a constant reaching out for more. This, then, comes first of all—something of a grasp, an ever-increasing grasp, of this marvellous old Book of God.

179

Some of us are a bit old-fashioned in these days. We believe there are books and *The Book*. If you have time for books and *The Book*, good! But if you are a bit busy, and have not all the time you might like to have for books and *The Book*, you must put books in a distinctly secondary place, and see that *The Book* of God has the very first place. This Book is not simply to teach us. It is for that, but it is for far more. It is a sword. It has a keen edge. As you use God's own Word you will find there is a power in the Word itself, apart from yourself, that goes home to men's hearts. And in these days, when the old Book is being discussed and dissected so much, it is well to remember that we are not to prove the Bible, but to use it. There are times when proving by explaining is useful and helpful. But the important thing, the chief thing, is to *use* it. Give God's Spirit a chance, through this marvellous weapon, to cut His own way into human hearts. And if you find sometimes that men are doubting the keenness of the edge of your sword, if they say, 'That bit of the edge there, that is not steel, that is a bit soft'; the thing for you and me to do is not to try and prove, except in an incidental way, that the sword is all right, but just to stick 'em with it, and they will quickly find out what a keen Damascus blade it is, and how well honed its edge is, all the time. The first essential, then, in the equipment for service is a grip upon this old Book. And I want to say this, allow nothing—if you would be true to our Master, and true to your fellows— allow nothing to steal away from you the daily bit of quiet time. I mean extra time planned for getting alone with the Book, absorbing it, to get full of it, to be freshened by it; because that is an essential, absolutely, in our equipment.

I love to say what I have said before and what I know

and believe more and more, the more I come into touch with sinful, needy men, I know it is true more and more —there is more than print here. There is print, and paper, and binding; and what is here must be gotten hold of through mental processes, in the natural order. But there is more than that, there is a Person here; there is a Spirit in these pages, a loving, keen, active Spirit. Let us use the old Book more, and trust Him who grips the handle of this marvellous sword.

But there is a second essential. And we are climbing up one step here. And this second thing is an essential; it is *a hot heart*. The shortest road into any man is through his heart. Sometimes you must—nay, very often—you must persuade a man's will. We are to approach men through their intelligence. God gave intelligence. But, mark this, the one short road everywhere is the heart road. We must have a heart that is hot! I do not mean a head that is hot. We ought to have this combination—a head like a refrigerator, and a heart like a furnace. Neither one nor the other, but one and the other.

But if you will mark it keenly, only as the Lord Jesus Christ is Master can we keep the line sharply marked between the two. If His mastery is not the real thing, one of two things will happen. And one of these two things is happening all the time. Either the coldness of the head gets into the heart—that is very common and very bad—or else the hotness of the heart gets up into the head, and that may be less common, and very bad. We want a cool head, as God planned. If God may have His way, it will be so. But the thing I am speaking of now is this, a hot heart, a heart that is full of warm blood. The heart decides the warmth of your hand, and the warmth of your feet, and the strength of your feet.

It is only as there is good heart action that there can be good circulation. A hot heart—good heart action—always means swift feet, tireless feet going everywhere, and going all the while.

And if the heart action is good, your hand will be warm. And of all the things you do not want in Christian service, it is a cold hand. A man in the Merrimac River was thrown overboard. I think the boat went down, and they were rescuing the people. It was winter-time, and somebody was shoving the edge of a plank out to this man. But the plank was covered with ice, and the ice was slippery. And as the man tried to take hold he could not. It was too cold and slippery. And by and by he mustered up strength to cry out, 'Please don't push the cold end to me.' Ah! from the great crowd all around us there is a great cry going out all the time, 'Don't push the cold end out to me; give me the warm end'. May we remember this—God has a heart! The heart of God broke on Calvary, because of His love for men. The Lord Jesus Christ was the heart of God reaching out to men. And wherever He has His way there will be a hot, tender heart, a full circulation of warm blood, and swift, tireless feet, and warm, clinging, tender hands. How hungry the crowd is to-day! In London, in New York, in all the world, it is hungry in its heart for the touch of love. That is the second essential—a hot heart, a God-touched heart, a God- swayed heart.

And the third thing is higher yet. It is this, *the Holy Spirit's power*. You have heard very much about that. The books are full of it, convention teaching is full of it; and yet, and yet, one needs to stop very often and remind himself of this—there is no power except as the Holy Spirit has continual sway. There is no power apart from Him. There may be a well-trained brain. There may

be a marvellous grasp of the old Book. There may
be a tender, sympathetic heart, and tireless running, and
very extended organisation—and what splendid organisation we have in Christian service in our day!—and yet
all of these things will fall utterly short, except the Holy
Spirit, the gift of our enthroned Jesus Christ, is allowed
to come in and take possession of our organisation, and
take possession of our brain, and take possession of the
body, and sway the whole as He may choose.

Do you remember the last time our Master was with
His disciples? I do not know whether it was evening-
time or morning, the old Book does not tell, but I have
fancied I could see the Master with the Eleven, one
morning, walking out of the city, down the old street,
through the gate, up the slope of the Hill of Olives.
Here is the Master, His face torn by the thorns and by
the thongs, marred by suffering as no man's face was
ever marred, but with a wondrous glory light. And here
is John, always near, but just a bit nearer, with a new
light in his face; and by his side there is another man
who one time followed afar off, and got into bad form.
But, you know, I think Peter is very close by his Master's
side, with a great love in his eye; for the Master forgave
his great break, and Peter's devotion, his love, shines
out of his great eyes. Thus they are walking along.
Our Master is talking, and they are keenly listening, with
an occasional question, as they climb Olivet's top. Two
things the Master is burning in. One is this, they are to
go on an errand. It is a life-errand, taking all their life-
power to the end of their lives. It is a world-errand.
They are to go, with all the strength and devotion they
have, out to men one by one, and to the uttermost parts
of the earth. That is the first thing—they are to go on
an errand, a life-errand.

The second thing is this, there is Somebody Else coming, who is to come upon them, and take possession of them, and guide them, and be their power. They are not to go till He comes. He will come, then they are to go. He who is coming would need them, and they who were going cannot do a thing without Him who is coming. That is to be the new partnership of service the Master says, for the world. The two. Shall I say, men and the Holy Spirit! Or, shall I say the Holy Spirit and men? I must say both; not we without Him, and—reverently— not He without us. We going and depending upon Him; He coming and working through us, and taking possession of us, and all the power His. He comes upon us, and He acts through us. He will strengthen the body, He will bring health to the body as the need may be; He will give life to the body for the service that needs to be done. He will guide our thinking; He will make the missionary keener to grasp the new language that must be gotten. He will guide the mental processes. He will teach you how to touch that man, and this man, differently. He will open the Book, He will simply be the life of one's mental powers. He guides through our mental pro- cesses; and only as we wait for Him, and listen to Him- self, and go only at His bidding, but go *at* His bidding, where He sends and when He sends and as He sends— just a keen, intelligent listening, and a wholehearted obedience—only so can there be that marvellous subtle thing that we call power. He acts through you. You will rise to talk to a crowd, and their faces are hard, and their hearts seem hard, and you cannot do a thing—some of us know that. Then as you quietly yield yourself, even while you are talking, there goes a something that changes the eyes, and bends the will. He comes, and opens the doors for you. He goes through that hardest thing of all to bend, the human will, and He opens the door hardest to open, the human heart. He can, and only He can, but He can. The Master's word is this: 'Tarry ye'. It would be a marvellous blessing many a time if we were to break some appointments. Now I am not telling you to break your appointments. An appointment is a sacred thing to be kept; if your word is passed, your honour is bound to it. Not to break appointments— but I say this, better by far break an appointment, let the preaching service go unpreached, and the people wondering, than go through the service, or keep the appointment, unless the Holy Spirit is resting upon you in power; better fewer services but more of His power. The Master said, 'Tarry ye. . . . Go ye'. Yes, tarry ye. The evenly-balanced law of the Christian life in service, is thus a continual going and tarrying. But here the word is this, 'Tarry, wait', to these men, 'until you have been clothed with power from on high.'

I want to ask you this: Have *you* received the Holy Spirit? You have been years in the service, you may have been faithful in the service, you may have done your work conscientiously, faithfully. Have you received the power of the Holy Spirit? Because I think some workers might well just turn aside, and cancel appointments for a bit, to tarry, and just stop, stop, and say: 'Have I yielded myself wholly to the sway of the Spirit of God?'

I want to suggest to you four simple words from the seventh chapter of John. If some friend here should ask, How may I receive the Holy Spirit—how may I have the power that shall be as subtle fire burning in me, and burning through my words and my service? I would just say over these four simple words. You know them very well. I shall not stop long on them. I am repeating them for my own sake. We have failed oftentimes. I have. Have you? Things have not always gone right with us; our hearts have been sore sometimes, and we have yearned for power. Let us go all back over the A B C again. How may I have this marvellous, subtle power of God, that shall burn and sway and melt in my service? Four simple words from the Master's lips, in John's seventh chapter, verses 37-39.

'On the last day, that great day of the Feast, Jesus stood and cried, saying, If any man thirst, let him come unto Me, and drink. He that believeth on Me, as the Scriptures saith, out of his inner being shall flow rivers of living water'. And then John explains, fifty or sixty years afterwards: 'This spake He of the Spirit which they that believe on Him were to receive; for the Holy Spirit was not yet come, because Jesus was not glorified.' The four words are these: Thirst, glorify, drink, believe.

Thirst—what does it mean? Intense desire. If you are thirsty, you cannot do anything till you have had a drink. Thirst simply means intensest desire. Are you thirsty? You workers, many of you, have been greatly blessed in your service. Are you thirsty? Have you had enough? 'I will pour water on him that is thirsty?' And if you are not thirsty, maybe you might be thirsty to be thirsty. Thirst for thirst. For there can be nothing before this. Thirsty! 'Blessed are they that thirst, for'—here is the promise for the thirsty—'they shall be filled'.

The second word is the word *Glorify*. You remember the historical meaning was this: Our Lord Jesus was down here in humiliation, rejected, crucified. He went back home, crucified by the earth, but crowned in heaven. When He got back home He was glorified— that is, He was crowned, He was enthroned, He was empowered. And the Holy Spirit coming down on that

Pentecost Day was the gift of a glorified Lord Jesus. The Spirit's Presence said this: 'The crucified Jesus, the absent Jesus, is a *glorified* Jesus'. The personal meaning is this: When you and I glorify Him, then we shall have the fulness of the power of the Holy Spirit. They glorified Him by enthroning Him; so must we. But the trouble is this: I found that my throne was occupied. How about yours? There had to be a *de*thronement before there could be an *en*thronement. Somebody else, something else was on the throne. And what the Master means here is this, that He must be enthroned as Master, that self must be starved, strangled, crucified. Only as self which occupies the throne is put out, and put to death, and the Lord Jesus Christ is put on the throne as Master only so can there be power. The whole rub is right there. To have the Master come in, for example, as King, enthroned, may mean this: He might say, I want you to bundle up your stuff and go to Africa. Oh, you had not thought of that! You thought of preaching fine sermons to people who could appreciate your scholarly attainments; and you will be true to your Master, of course, in that preaching. But that was rather your own plan, with your University training, and your culture and polish. Africa! Savages for you! But there is a Lord of the harvest. The secret of power is in the sovereignty of our Lord. When He says Africa, you say: 'Yes, Master,' and pack your box and look up the railroad schedule. He might mean that you should not go to Africa as you planned, or India as you planned. Sometimes there is a bit of a glamour over the foreign field; but just to throw yourself away, as some would say, in that common humdrum slum section—oh! no glamour about that.

He might say: 'I want you to take that wealth that has

come to you, and let Me have the use of it, and I will take care of you'. Oh! that's the last thing we part with— money. Consecration seems to reach the purse last. Somebody said that in a consecration 'personal' ought to be spelled 'purse and all'. But it means simply this, that you say: 'Lord Jesus Christ, here is my throne. Take possession of it. I cannot put that self off. Put it off. I am not my own. Take possession, and my whole life shall be gladly at Thy beck and call'. That is the meaning of the word glorify. And I think one reason why there is a lack of power is simply this. We understand all that; you can tell it to me maybe better than I can tell it you, dear reader; but the thing is to *do* it, to put Him there and keep Him there, because there is power only as there is a glorified Lord Jesus in the heart and in the life.

The third word is the word *Drink*. It simply means 'take'. You know drinking is just the easiest process in all the world. You simply tip the glass—no agonising, no pleading, but you just take it. And here it simply means this: 'Lord Jesus Christ, I am so thirsty for Thy power, and I surrender all. I make Thee my Lord, an absolute autocrat. I take from Thee the Holy Spirit. Thank You.' Is that all? Yes. 'I do not feel any different!' It is not a matter of feeling, it is His Word. 'He that believeth, out of his inner being shall flow'. Just take. I accept!

And the fourth word is the word *Believe*. It means this, expect, expect. Thirst, desire, enthronement, expect, expect. It means this, that as you go out in your service feeling no different, to speak a message, you are to expect that as you speak the quiet word to the old crowd there will be a new fire burning. Whatever service may come, expect, expect. You know power is always manifest in action. I might tell you that I had power enough to lift a chair in my one hand, and you would say, 'Well, it looks as if you had power enough to do that'. My hand may be defective. But I take the chair up, and now you know there is that much power. Power is always manifest in action. And as we go, just in the old round, through the old alleys, through the old treadmill, expect. Say, 'Master, Thou art on the throne; and I know the power will come'. Expect! And, mark you, this power will come and will go, until there will be far more than you are conscious of. It is not the promise of consciousness of power; we are oftentimes hungry for that. We like our emotions stirred. No! He promises power; and as you write the letter, or lead the service, or have the personal touch, or do this and that, the power of God will go out of you, and the fire will burn, and the results will come. You will know some of the results. But, mark you, a man of real power is always least conscious of the power there is in his life.

May this be our prayer:

> My glorious Victor, Prince Divine,
> Clasp these surrendered hands in Thine;
> At length my will is all Thine own,
> Glad vassal of a Saviour's throne.
>
> My Master, lead me to Thy door;
> Pierce this now willing ear once more:
> Thy bonds are freedom; let me stay
> With Thee, to toil, endure, obey.
>
> Yes, ear and hand, and thought and will,
> Use all in Thy dear slav'ry still!
> Self's weary liberties I cast
> Beneath Thy feet; there keep them fast.

Tread them still down; and then I know,
These hands shall with Thy gifts o'erflow;
And piercèd ears shall hear the tone
Which tells me Thou and I are one.

Bishop Moule